The Tailor and Ansty

D0019522

The Tailor and Ansty

ERIC CROSS

With an Introduction by FRANK O'CONNOR and a
Postscript giving the Tailor's views on the banning of this
book

THE MERCIER PRESS
4 BRIDGE STREET, CORK

First published in 1942
Second Edition 1964
© 1942 by Eric Cross
This edition 1970
Reprinted 1972

Reprinted 1975
Printed by The Kerryman Ltd.,
Tralee, Co. Kerry, Eire.

SBN 85342 050 5

Introduction to the 1964 Edition

When I wrote the introduction to the original edition of *The Tailor and Ansty* the models were still alive. They were a remarkable old couple who lived in a tiny cottage on the mountain road up to the lake at Gougane Barra. On fine days you found the Tailor sitting by the roadside, "standing to the cow", as his wife called it. I should, perhaps, say The Cow, for like everything else about the Tailor it had a tendency to turn into capital letters. He was a small, crippled man with a round, merry face. Neighbours, visitors and students would pause for a chat with him; students because he spoke beautiful Irish, visitors because they found his English conversation entertaining enough. It was, though it was not as good as his Irish conversation. In Irish he had a whole field of folk stories and songs to fall back on, with the elegance of an older world about it; in English he had no such models for style. At the same time, English extended his mind over a wider range of subjects, and, in spite of his lack of worldly experience, he had a good mind, shrewd and inquisitive. He was, as I described him in life, a rural Dr Johnson.

Ansty was a beautiful woman who looked like the Muse of Tragedy but talked like a quite different muse. For a long time she was a pin-up girl, made famous in Christmas cards and calendars by a photographer who showed her in her West Cork cloak, bringing in the yule log. She wanted to know at once whether or not you were married and how many children you had, and if you failed to come up to her standards of sexual performance offered you "the loan of my ould shtal's breeches". To her, all men were "shtals" – stallions – including her husband, and it offended her nice sense of propriety to see a young woman who was not in the way of breeding. She and the Tailor both regarded sexual relations as the most entertaining subject for general conversation; a feature of life in Irish-speaking Ireland even in my youth, but which began to die out the moment English became the accepted language. The Tailor's comment on the rise of Fascism was that "There wouldn't be half this trouble if more people fell to breeding" – in which he may have been wiser than we know. He never changed the tone of his conversation before women or children, and I noticed that he had a genuine dislike of anything mealy-mouthed. One night, I was recording a beautiful love song from his friend, Batty Kit, and, because Father Traynor was with me, Batty boggled at a verse. "Go on! Go on!" the Tailor snapped in Irish. "You didn't write it or compose it." To him, a song or story was something that had been transmitted with a purpose, and it was great impertinence on anyone's part to alter it. Nancy MacCarthy overheard a conversation between himself and another old man after the banning of my translation of Merriman's "Midnight Court". Both of them knew that very long poem in Irish, and the neighbour argued that "There were many things in it he wouldn't like little boys and girls to be reading" – the Puritan whine. The Tailor grew angry. "You can't know a man and know only half of him. If you want to know a man you must know the whole of him, and it should never have been banned – all of it must go in." Ansty's tongue in particular was dreaded by respectable women in the neighbourhood. "Oh, Gaad, she's aaful; she'd shame 'oo!" one respectable woman said to me about her. The old couple were virtuous; they were not respectable, and they paid dearly for it.

Outside the neighbourhood they had a wide group of friends. There were Father Traynor, known as the "Saint", a young priest from Dublin; Nancy MacCarthy, the chemist from Cork, Seamus Murphy, the sculptor, Ripley (pronounced "Ruppley"), an American journalist and his wife; somebody called "The English Colonel", whose name I never ascertained, Kirsten, the Danish girl, and of course, "Crass", the author of this book. Once, when Ripley had had an operation at the American Hospital in Paris, I saw the old couple weeping, Ansty quite without restraint. Everything that concerned these friends they regarded as a personal matter. "So-and-so inwited the Ruppleys to dinner," Ansty said angrily to me, "and whin they gat there he gave them nathing but ould vine to drink, and no fushkey at aall!"

It is hard to describe what constitutes charm in a married couple but they had it. Like The Cow, their marriage should probably be described in capital letters. They were Man and Woman, forever squabbling and making up, eternally equal and separate; Ansty always anxious, busy, concrete, the Tailor always placid, indolent and abstract. When there were visitors she rarely sat down but bustled about the end of the room, dusting, sweeping, replacing. One night the Tailor, trying to quiet her down, quoted at her what the Gárlach Coileánach said of his mother: "My mother will have been drowned a year tomorrow – she'd have been round the lake since then."

6

When Mr Cross's book appeared all of us who knew the Tailor and Ansty were delighted. Our Dr Johnson had at last found his Boswell. The reviews were enthusiastic and Nancy MacCarthy brought them out to read by the fire. Nancy describes "the look of shy pleasure" in Ansty's face whenever a reviewer referred favourably to The Cow.

But we were all too innocent to anticipate the effect the book would have on Mr de Valera's well-educated government. It was banned as being "in its general tendency indecent". I didn't mind their saying that about my own work. After all, you don't take up a dangerous trade like literature in Ireland without developing the hide of a rhinoceros and renting a house in a strategic spot with direct access to the sea. What alarmed me was that the Tailor and Ansty lived in a mountain townland where people still believed in the fairies. It wasn't only an unpleasant situation; it could be a dangerous one.

It strained my patience and Traynor's, and, compared with me, he was in a hopeless position. I could say what I liked, and did, while he, whose relationship to the old couple was more like that of a son than of a friend, dared not, as a Catholic priest, open his mouth in public in their defence.

The man who did was a Protestant landlord, Sir John Keane, who tabled a motion in the Senate condemning the Censorship Board. Everyone interested either in censorship or in Irish public life would do well to get hold of the four day debate in the Senate Proceedings for 1943. Reading it is like a long, slow swim through a sewage bed.

Keane insisted on reading from the book over the impassioned protests of the other senators who dreaded – it is on record – that pornographers would buy the proceedings of the Irish Senate as an anthology of evil literature, and that prize collection of half-wits ordered the quotations to be struck from the record.

The principal spokesman for the Government was Professor William Magennis of the National University. Magennis was at one time the Government's choice as their representative on the Board of the Abbey Theatre, and Yeats replied angrily that he would close the theatre rather than allow such a man on to its board. Instead, Magennis was made a member of the Censorship Board. "Gifted with a mighty intellect and a great store of knowledge," said one lady senator, "he could, if personal ambition had been his guiding star, have stayed in his study and written one of those great philosophical works that would have made his name shine forever." The effect of the tribute is slightly weakened by another statement of the same lady, that "If Dante could come to life again and wanted to think of a really cruel

7

punishment for his political enemies, if he condemned them for all eternity to read a book like *The Tailor and Ansty* there could not be any torture that would get at their 'innards' more fiercely."

Magennis dominated the debate. He was a windbag with a nasty streak of malice, and in a torrent of irrelevancies interspersed with innuendoes he tried to drown the opposition he could not reply to. Of the characters of this book he said, "The man is sex-obsessed. His wife, Anastasia – called here 'Ansty' – is what in the language of American psychology is called a moron – a person of inferior mental development who may be thirty or forty years of age, but has reached only the mental age of a child of four or five." Magennis knew what lay behind it all. "There is a campaign going on in England to undermine Christianity. It is financed by American money. The society that is the main agent in the endeavour to put in paganism instead of the Christian creed and practice includes Professor Joad and George Bernard Shaw."

I should strain my reader's credulity too much if I quoted from the speeches of Mr Fitzgerald, Mr Foran, Mr Counihan, Mr Callaghan, Mr Quirke and Mr Hayes. The division showed only Sir John Keane and his reluctant seconder by courtesy in favour of his motion. One could hardly imagine a completer defeat. Yet, within ten years the Censorship Board had to be reconstructed much more drastically than Keane ever imagined possible, and one of the first books discovered not to be obscene was the very one that was so obscene that it could not even be quoted in the records of the House!

But the Tailor and Ansty had to live through it all. To all intents and purposes they were boycotted. Each week, Guard Hoare, an old friend of theirs, cycled out to see them from Ballingeary – a warning to hooligans. One afternoon three priests appeared and forced the old man on to his knees at his own hearth and made him burn his copy of the book – "eight and sixpence worth" as Ansty said to me. To her, eight and sixpence was an awful lot of money.

Traynor and I motored down to see them, and when we were leaving we found the front door jammed. Some hooligans had jammed the branch of a tree between the latch and the wall, and Jackie, their son, had to climb through the little window to release us. Ansty was hysterical, and the Tailor patted her gently. "Easy, girl, easy!" he whispered. "At our age there is little the world can do to us."

I only saw him once again before he died, and though the house was empty but for ourselves, he talked as well as I had ever heard him do. Soon after, he fell ill. Ansty told Nancy

MacCarthy, "The divil was ever reddening the pipe, God rest him, and I used to be scolding him for fear he'd fire the bed." The old neighbours decided to ignore the disgrace he had brought upon them all and Ansty made a sour comment on the way they drank up her good tea. At the funeral next day she made ribald ones on the men who attended. That night the men sat round the fire as they used to do in the old days and swapped stories about the Tailor. There was general agreement that the great tragedy of the whole business was that at the very time the Tailor died, Guard Hoare was gallantly cycling out all the way from Ballingeary with a bottle of whisky for him. The bottle of whisky he had not drunk had cast a gloom over the proceedings. Suddenly, Ansty, who as usual was fussing about by the door with her broom, rested her arms on it and said, "There'll be great talk Above tonight." It had suddenly dawned on her that her own loss was Heaven's happiness.

She died herself in the hospital in Cork, forty miles away, still believing herself at home and inquiring anxiously of visitors if Johnny Con was "standing to the cow".

She and the Tailor are buried together under a beautiful tombstone designed by Seamus Murphy in the graveyard at Gougane Barra. A short distance away, Tim Traynor has been buried on the island. No monument to him has been permitted, but his friends have drawn his initials on the ground in pebbles. But, for those who remember them today, the echo of their innocent laughter is not in Gougane Barra but in the pages of Eric Cross's book. The written word remains.

FRANK O'CONNOR

Chapter One

"In the townland of Garrynapeaka, in the district of Inchigeela, in the parish of Iveleary, in the barony of West Muskerry, in the county of Cork, in the province of Munster" – as he magniloquently styles his address, lives the Tailor.

His small whitewashed cottage, with its acre of ground, stands at the brow of a hill, at the side of a road which winds and climbs into a deep glen of the mountains bordering Cork and Kerry.

In the summer you will usually find the Tailor himself leaning up against the bank of the road, minding his one black cow. As you pass up the hill he will have watched you come and sized you up in his shrewd and kindly way. As he stands talking to you, helping you, pointing out this and that to you, you will scarcely believe that he has seventy-seven years put over him. The vigour of his body, in spite of the handicap of his crutch, the firm tones of his voice, the smile of his lively eyes, the thick head of silver hair, all belie the fact of the years.

He will most likely invite you inside for a glass of buttermilk or a heat of the tea. Go with him. Let the beauties of Ireland wait. They will still be there when he has gone. Be, as he is, prodigal of time, and sit and listen to him. Forget the rest of your journey as the Tailor forgets the cow. Humanity matters more than either cattle or scenery. You have met a man – finished.

Sit by his turf fire at night and learn how to practise his favourite precept – "Glac bog an saoghal agus glachgig an saoghal bog tu: Take the world fine and aisy and the world will take you fine and aisy." And that other one of his: "The world is only a blue bag. Knock a squeeze out of it when you can."

You have met a man who has lived to the utmost within his limits. A man who has grown and learned and become wise and splendidly tolerant and full of a sense of fun. Someone whom St Francis, Montaigne, Rabelais, Shakespeare and his Falstaff would have loved – richly human. First of all human, and the rest – Irish, Catholic, tailor – afterwards.

Always he has suffered the handicap of a withered leg and has hobbled through life with a crutch and a stick. He has

10

treated that as a mere bagatelle and brushed it aside with an air of contemptuous indifference as he has treated so many of the details of life. Actually, indeed, it has proved little handicap to his activity. He has managed to find his way all over the mountains of West Cork and Kerry. He has travelled distances by road which would tire a strong man with two sound legs. He has managed to travel beyond his own country, and still at seventy-seven clambers up the rocks of his little acre for a vantage-point for the herding of his cow.

Now he does little travelling. "The heart is playing at him." His journeyings are limited to Garrynapeaka, apart from an occasional excursion by car. He does not worry. Garrynapeaka is a mirror of the rest of the world. The road runs through it, and those who travel the road – neighbours on their way to a fair, the local guards, visitors in the summer – all drop into him. On winter nights his kitchen is always full. He learns all the news, all the gossip, all the scandal, and what happens in Iveleary is, after all, of deeper concern to him than the doubtful headline reports from Outer Mongolia which we call news. He is content now to be a great traveller in Garrynapeaka, as another wise man was "content to have travelled much in Concord".

He has received an old age pension of ten shillings a week since he was seventy. He takes great glee in the fact that, to date, he has managed to get £150 from the Government "free, gratis and for nothing". He remarks on the fact that his mother lived to be ninety-eight, and if she had been drawing "the pension" she would have drawn over seven hundred pounds! He chuckles at the possibility of his own achievement of that age. It is not the greed for money. He is contemptuous of money. It is the sense of fun of the thing.

Though he is tailor by trade as well as by name to all who know him, he has not practised the craft seriously for many years. But his interest in the trade remains. He will offer "to build a suit" for you, but you would need the patience of Job to see the end of the job. He will study the cut of your clothes. He will finger the stuff of which they are made, and his tradesman's pride is roused at the sight of a missing button.

He will readily offer to put a stitch in something for you, or to sew on a button or to patch a wearing garment. The job, however, will be incidental to the talk. He will hold you a prisoner by a needle and thread or to ransom in your shirt sleeves. The button sewing may take an hour's combined labour and talk. A puckish sense of fun runs through it all. If it should be an alpaca jacket which is at fault the Tailor will invariably patch it with a piece of broadcloth. If the missing button is black

11

you may be certain that the one he sews on will be white. In his own phrase – "They serve the purpose. What harm?"

He can be serious withal, and give a considered opinion or discuss any topic you may care to introduce. But life is too short for a long face. Soon his eyes will twinkle, the corners of them will wrinkle, his lips will tremble and he will burst into a chuckle which grows to a rollicking, room-filling laugh at the thought of some incident which has invaded and tickled his mind.

"Keep all the fun to yourself, of course!" breaks in the scornful voice of Ansty.

Ansty is the obverse of the medal – The Tailor and Ansty. She is his wife or, as he refers to her, "his bitter half, his misfortune". In almost all aspects they differ, yet each is incomplete without the other. They are Jack Spratt and his wife. Between them they lick the platter of life clean.

The Tailor finds some good content in the worst day of the winter. Ansty finds some fault in the best day that the summer ever brings. The Tailor sits, Silenus-like, upon his butter-box by the side of the fire, with fun and interest dancing in his eyes. Ansty wanders in and out of the house, broom in hand, hair awry, looking like one of the Furies and acting as an antithetical chorus to the Tailor's view of life.

The Tailor greets you at first sight with warmth. Not so Ansty. For a long time she will view you with a searching and sceptical eye. The Tailor treats the dog and the cat as friends and talks to them. Ansty spends half her day hunting them with her broom, and cursing them with her tongue. If they are in they ought to be out. If they are out they ought to be in.

"Pigs where hens ought to be. Hens where pigs ought to be. Ten o'clock in the morning, and not a child washed yet in the house. The whole world is upside down!" comments the Tailor with mock wonder from his corner.

Again, the fire is always too big and wasteful for Ansty, or else too small and miserable. For the Tailor – there's a fire on the hearth. "God's in His heaven. All's right with the world."

The Tailor is interested in everything under the sun, and his mind, like a bee, sucks the nectar of every notion, whereas Ansty is interested in nothing but her immediate surroundings and the echoes which linger in her mind without interest. The Tailor will return tomorrow to a point discussed today with a freshly remembered instance or a pertinent story. He has a sense of continuity and flow. Ansty's thought and interest are a series of full stops and exclamations. An hour after a subject has been mentioned, she echoes a phrase of it, inconsequentially as she wanders in and out of the cottage:

"Domson wine! . . . The Lord save us! . . . Domson wine! . . . Glory be! . . . Domson wine! . . . Ring a dora! Domson wine! . . . Iosa Christe!"

The Tailor pauses in his discourse and cocks his ear for a moment, and then turns to Ansty with a serious inquiry.

"Tell me – is that a new saint that you and the Pope made this morning, that you are so busy saying your prayers to?"

Ansty, by the way, is an abbreviation of Anastasia, and the Tailor's official name is "Mr Buckley", but they are known always as "The Tailor and Ansty".

Ansty has a hard life, made even harder by her own nature. Most of the work of the place falls upon her, and her overture to most of the day's reminiscences begins with, "Wisha! when I got up this morning, very early entirely, to let out the cow, and himself still shno-o-o-ring away in the bed like an ould pig, or a gintleman—"

Her life is a round of worries. She is at the mercy of every most trivial circumstance. She is full of fears for her ducks and hens from the passing motors and the fox and the rats. The rabbits will destroy the cabbage in the garden. The rain will destroy the turf. Then when all these everyday worries are banished there still remain the thunders and the fairies.

The Tailor sits in his corner, the master of circumstance and captain of his soul. If the roof fell in upon him he would but shake himself, and straightaway remember a case of similar occurrence and some curious story attached to the happening.

Ansty is direct and spontaneous in her thoughts and the expression of them. She uses the same earthy language to whomsoever she may be talking, regardless of their attitude, and she revels a little in the surprise and shock which she often produces. A twinkle comes to her eye at the least sign of your discomfiture. You do well to keep a poker face for Ansty. The Tailor adapts himself both in his speech and his subject matter to his listener, and in all ways endeavours to please.

"Listen to the to-o-one of him, will you?" interjects Ansty. "You'd think it was to the Pope himself he was talking, he's so grand."

Both are fluent Irish speakers. The Tailor is somewhat of an authority on the language, but has little patience with the hot-house cultivation or revival of the language, to which he refers with scorn as "the boiling programme" (bi-lingual programme). They share a genius, too, for the coining and the use of strange words, which, until you have become accustomed to them, are as a foreign language. They use them, play with them, and do not worship them. Seldom do they refer to anyone by their familiar names. Each has a nickname of their own invention, so that a conversation between them is often a series of riddles to an outsider.

The Tailor both reads and writes. Both of these arts are profound mysteries to Ansty, and she treats them with respect as though they were arts of the devil. On the occasions when the Tailor is stirred to correspondence, Ansty assists as Acolyte. The table is erected and carefully wiped. Ansty bears in, from the Room, the box containing the stationery, the pen and bottle of ink, and then sits silently and watches and waits.

The Tailor fishes out whatever flies have drowned themselves in the ink-bottle, and then braces himself for the job. First of all he must find the address of his correspondent. If that is not immediately forthcoming, it is always enough excuse for deferring the task until tomorrow.

He has been caught several times in some sort of trap, and has developed a deep suspicion of the whole postal service. After all his labours letters have been returned to him undelivered. He has grown wary now and usually gets someone else to address the envelopes, for his own version of addresses does not always comply with regulations. He is quite indifferent as to where he puts his own or his correspondent's. Sometimes his own will be on the envelope.

He tells the story about his own experience, when he was asked to write a letter by some woman to her brother in America. "After spending a piece of the night at the job, I asked her for the address to which the letter was to be sent. 'Oh, just address it to Micky Sullivan, Rocky Mountains, America!' said she."

Occasionally the Tailor will deign to read the paper to Ansty. Again it is the mystery of the art which entrances her. The folds are pressed out of the paper. The Tailor puts on his spectacles; as a matter of form, not because his eyes need them. Ansty sits bolt upright, tense with attention. The Tailor chooses an account of the meeting of the County Council and begins.

"At Clonakilty, on the first of June—"

"Wisha!" exclaims Ansty, with a voice filled with wonder. "At Clonakilty? . . . Glory be! . . . On the first of June? . . . The Lord save us! . . . That for 'oo! . . . On the first of June, at Clonakilty!" She will continue to orchestrate on a couple of phrases and her exclamations and silence without paying any further attention to the content of the reading. Then suddenly the charm is broken. She will whirl up from the chair like a tornado, at the sound of a cart or footsteps on the road – and the ceremony is brought to an abrupt finish. Life is more important than news.

Ansty's world is very limited and personal. Bantry and

Macroom come within the compass of it. Cork is a strain upon her imagination. Beyond Cork lies the rest of the world, and Heaven and Hell. When the labours of the day are ended she can still sit and listen to the Tailor talking with fresh wonder, though she must have heard most of it until she knows it by heart herself.

But only at night, by the fire, does she show this respect for him. During the day it is otherwise. The Tailor may be sitting, contentedly expounding some point or other, while perhaps the rain lashes down outside. Ansty comes in. She leans on her broom for a moment. The rain drips from her. Then she will interrupt him with contempt.

"Hmph! You – sitting there with your bottom in the ashes discussing 'feelosophy' and the rain slashin' in at the door!"

The Tailor simulates anger at the interruption.

"Thon amon dieul!" (T-anam an diabhal – your soul to the devil.) "What would you have me do? Do you want me to sit with my bottom to the door to keep the rain out?"

For many, many years, Ansty has worn, on weekdays, the same clothes, until she has become, as the Tailor describes her, "more like a blessed bush at a holy well than a woman", so tattered are her clothes. Yet the Tailor vows that she has a goodly stock of clothes upstairs – "the grandest museum of clothes you ever did see. There'll be a great auction at her wake, for some of the dresses are so old that their like no longer exists in the world today. They are so old that they have been in and out of fashion twice already."

On Sundays and holy days, however, Ansty surprises you. She combs up her Medusa-like hair, and puts on her black West Cork cloak with the hood thrust back. Then you realize that she was once the beauty of the neighbourhood, and beneath the filigree of wrinkles is still beautiful; still, in spite of the sharpness of her tongue, is delicate and feminine. Her eyes seem to regain the blue of the skies, and her hair, now tamed, you see is still golden amidst the silver. She is so changed that you might think her everyday self a pose, so that her Sunday self may always startle you.

Sunday is her high day. She goes to Mass and meets all the people she knows, and talks to them all in her racy manner. The Tailor stays at home and minds the house. All days are high days and holidays to him. "Come day. Go day. Let's have another day." But on Sundays he changes his shirt and wears the black hat at a different angle.

All these comparisons are only comparisons of surfaces and appearances. Beneath all the seeming asperity of her appearance Ansty has a heart as big as the Tailor's. After the period of the rigour of her scrutiny and the shrewishness of her tongue, Ansty has an affection as great, a gratitude as deep, a kindliness as gentle as has the Tailor. Her home and all that she has and all that she can do for you are yours, gladly given, for Ansty and the Tailor, though they are two aspects of the same medal, are made of the same metal.

Chapter Two

The whitewashed cottage of Garrynapeaka is, in outward appearance, much like all such cottages built under the Labourers' Cottage Act. It contains four rooms, two upstairs – the Loft – and two downstairs.

The heart of the place is the open fireplace with a black, sooty crane and the pot-hooks hanging from it, and the fire which never dies. At night the embers of the fire are smoored with ashes and in the morning are uncovered again and kindled into flame with chips of "fir", the dried resinous wood from the bottom of the bogs.

The Tailor acts as Vesta. For years, until it has become a delicate art, he has tended and watched and nursed this heart of the house. He takes a great delight in astonishing you with his skill, and will let the fire die down until Ansty is almost speechless with wrath, and you, the spectator, imagine that at last the fire must be relit and the hearth desecrated with a match.

Slowly, so that you are the more impressed, the Tailor sets to work.... He rakes the last embers to the front. Methodically he builds a wall of sods of turf at the back and then feeds a few splinters of "fir" and small pieces of turf to the faint embers and stacks more turf about them. A few subtle wafts from his hat, neither too gentle nor too vigorous, and presto! there is a lively leaping fire again and a twinkle in the tailor's eye at the sight of your wondering approbation.

Only once, some years ago when he discarded his cap for the Saint's soft black hat, did he almost fail. Almost but not quite. The ritual had been performed almost to the last. Only the wafting remained to be done. He took off the new black hat and fanned the pile with it. There was no response. He fanned harder, but it looked as though he was beaten.

Hurling the hat from him in disgust he seized the old cap again and the fire responded immediately.

"The divil mend it! Whatever powers a priest may have they are not in his hat."

Since then he has developed the technique with the hat, and all is well.

By the side of the road there is a rick of turf for the fire and a pile of "fir" for the kindling. All through the day the fire is busy, for all the cooking is done upon it and Ansty is always boiling water for tea or for the cow or for washing. In the winter, when the dark days come and the nights are long, there are logs to be burnt with a glow and a crackle, while the neighbours sit round and smoke, and the Tailor supplies them with entertainment far richer than money could buy.

At one side of the fire is an upturned butter-box. This is the Tailor's fireside seat. It is placed so that its opening is between his legs, and here he sits, never upon a chair.

Like everything else in the house it has a name. The Tailor refers to it always as "Cornucopia" and explains that a long time ago a Greek king gave such a box to a "jolly cupper", who gave him a drink when he was thirsty, telling her that whenever she was in the want of anything she had but to look inside and she would find it there.

"Glory be!" chimes Ansty. "Anything she wanted! Ring a dora!"

"Yes, anything she wanted," raps back the Tailor, "but like all women she needed sense most of all but did not know it."

For a moment Ansty is beaten, but immediately rallies.

"Did she look for a man in it?" she asks, with a leer.

"She did," replies the Tailor. "Didn't I tell you there was anything she wanted inside in it?"

"Aha!" laughs Ansty, "that for 'oo! She found a man in it!" Then after a moment's silence, while her victory sinks in, her mood changes. "The divil mend you! you don't fall into it yourself, the way you spend the day and the night with your backside glued to it, like an old statoo!"

To tell the strict truth, the Tailor does periodically fall into it. He estimates that a butter-box lasts him about three years and then collapses beneath him. But it is never changed until it fails. He enjoys the element of danger and surprise. Besides, it would break a ritual.

Whatever Amalthea's horn held, the Tailor's "Cornucopia" almost rivals it for contents. Beneath the axe with the insecure head, with which he chops wood upon the hearthstone, and the goose-wing with which he sweeps up the ashes, there is a collection of bits of cloth, cords, tins, bits of tools and such-like things, out of which he can always find a makeshift for almost anything.

Across the hearth, opposite to this, is the chair of honour. Once upon a time it was a chair, but age and usage have worn down the legs unevenly till the seat of it is only a stool's height from the floor and its centre of gravity differs from that of all chairs. The back of it is loose and the brace of the back holds a bent and jagged piece of iron, held with four bent nails. To sit on it successfully, without being hurled to the floor, is a feat of no mean dexterity. To rise from it without a jag or a tear is almost a miracle. The Tailor always bows the most favoured guest to it as though it was a throne.

There are other chairs, strong chairs, sound chairs, even new chairs, about the house, but those are only for minor guests in the Tailor's order of precedence. If you visit him alone, perforce you sit in the chair of honour. Ladies, too, have this preference. Ansty sits there in the evenings and does not give way to locals. If several people are visiting, the order of precedence is arranged, with a masterly courtesy, by a wave of the hand and a word. Ansty wipes the seats of the other chairs with a definitely wet cloth and retires to the settle. Cornucopia is sacrosanct. No one ever violates it. Even Ansty, no matter how weary, would not dare to sit upon it. What would happen if she did there is no telling and ho use in wondering. It would simply be akin to the sun not rising or black being white.

There are times, however, when the Tailor's diplomacy is swept aside by Ansty's more abrupt methods. If a guest should already be installed in the chair of honour and a guest of higher rank arrives, Ansty will simply and directly command, "Get up, 'oo, and give the chair to So-and-so."

Over the fireplace is "the clevy", a shelf filled with tins. One contains sugar and another tea. There is a box of pepper and one containing caraway seeds, which Ansty mixes with tea. The remainder of the tins are mysteries. Never during any operation in the economy of the house are they opened. Never is their contents appealed to as an illustration. Perhaps they are but tins without contents and simply are, as the collection of dishes and plates on the dresser, awaiting an occasion still buried in the future.

In the middle of "the clevy" is a cardboard box. That, too, has its mystery. It is a mystery, however, which has been revealed, or partly revealed. For it contains the clock, shut away from sight and dust, but whether it is a protection from sight or from dust is part of the mystery, for it is never consulted.

Behind "Cornucopia", against the wall, is the settle. In the corner of this, directly behind the Tailor, is the Office. This is his accumulation of correspondence over the years. There are letters, photos, postcards from all over the world, stacked up into a pile. Here, too, is his box of cuttings from papers. There are paragraphs cut from newspapers relating to people he knows mixed up with accounts of freak calves and such-like wonders. Between the arm of the settle and the wall are his pipes. Each pipe, each letter and each photo recalls a friend.

Sometimes the Tailor will stretch himself at his ease on the settle. His head will rest in the Office, "amongst his friends", and the correspondence will become a little more muddled after his repose than it was before, and the next time that he wants to show you a letter it will be more difficult to find it, "but, what harm? There is always tomorrow."

By the door as you come in stands the dresser with its stock of ware. Just as Cornucopia is the Tailor's preserve so is this Ansty's preserve. The Tailor never goes near it. Twice a year the settle and the dresser and the doors and the shutters of the windows are painted by Ansty until by now the accumulation of paint must be near to half an inch thick.

The Tailor never gives a hand, and views it all with cynical amusement. The only good that he can see in it is that it keeps the paint manufacturers busy and makes them rich. Ansty sees it in a very different light. It is a part of her round of worry. The house must be clean in case she should die tomorrow and the place not be ready for her wake. The Tailor's view is the more practical, for during the period of "giving the place a rough dash", as he calls it, he has no peace. He is hounded from one place to another, and wherever he goes seems to be just the one place Ansty wants to paint or whitewash. Then he does seem to get a lot of the paint and the wash on to himself, too, before it ends and it looks as though he really did all the work.

Above the settle, on the wall, hang some religious pictures and the little red lamp of the Sacred Heart and the wall lamp for the night. The care of the lamps is one of the Tailor's duties. At about the same time each day he takes down the two lamps, unscrews them, refills them, and cleans the glass chimneys and replaces them for the night.

Beyond the kitchen is The Room. Ansty speaks of it always in capital letters. The Tailor, however, refers to it as his studio. It does at least contain the tools of his trade. There is the sewing machine, which has not been used for years. Never since the day when he took some part out of it, and Ansty lost it before he had time to replace it, and the Tailor took that as a sign that the days of his serious work were over. There is also a pressing-board and a goose-iron and a collection of patterns of cloth.

Ansty makes more use of the Room. Here she keeps her pans of milk for cream and the churn for the butter-making. There is, too, a collection of the years, of odds and ends. The Tailor is little interested in the place and very seldom goes into it. It is a museum of the past, and the reality of the past lies in his own mind and not in mere things.

Upstairs are the bedroom, with a great box-bed, and the small room beyond where Ansty keeps the meal and corn so that even at night when she is asleep she can still guard it from the pilfering of the rats and the mice.

The whitewashed cottage, which is a landmark from the hills about, stands in an acre of thin-soiled, mountainy land. It is set with potatoes and a little hay and oats and cabbage. In the middle of it tower two huge ivy-covered rocks which provide a vantage-point for the Tailor when he is "minding the dairy herd", and for the more practically minded Ansty, make an excellent place for the drying and the bleaching of her wash.

Neighbours give them help with the small labour of ploughing and digging and reaping, and come gladly. A day with the Tailor is reward enough. No one passes the road without paying a call. Very seldom does a night pass, summer or winter, that some one at least, and more often several, do not drop in for the nightly "scoruiocht" at the Tailor's.

They are known and loved for miles around. Wherever you go in West Muskerry you hear "The Tailor and Ansty! They're an airy couple!"

Chapter Three

Come down to the Tailor's and hear himself talk. Wet or fine, early or late, alone or with a crowd, there's a welcome awaits you. Across the door of Garrynapeaka there is another world, where values are different; where there is still a zest for the details of living; where time no longer matters; where there is much laughter and little harm; and mixed with the laughter, wisdom and a fresh sense of reality, a man is judged by himself alone, and not by his position or his title, or his own sense of self-importance.

There is the sound of someone singing. Look over the half-door and listen and wait for a moment. The Tailor is sitting on Cornucopia, for once in a while plying his needle and singing away to himself. The ply of the needle fits the song, not the song the ply of the needle.

John Riordan was well known in Muskerry
  For soldering old iron and the fastening of shoes,
And all the old ladies in the range of the valley
  Knew the click of his hammer on their Ticky-Tack-Toos.
Micky, sing fal-de-dal, al-de-dal, al-de-dal,
  Micky, sing fal-de-dal all the day long,
And all the old ladies repaired to the smithy
  For fear that their Ticky-Tack-Toos would go wrong.

A tinker's old lady repaired to the smithy,
  Saying there was a hole in her galley-pot blue.
When Micky beheld it he said he could weld it
  By adding a piece to her Ticky-Tack-Too.
Micky, sing fal-de-dal, al-de-dal, al-de-dal,
  Micky, sing fal-de-dal all the day long,
And all the old ladies repaired to the smithy
  For fear that their Ticky-Tack-Toos would go wrong.

The tinker came in while the job was in motion
  And right then at Micky his hammer he drew,
"By the bones of his father," he said, "he would rather
  Himself patch and solder her Ticky-Tack-Too."

Micky, sing fal-de-dal, al-de-dal, al-de-dal,
  Micky, sing fal-de-dal, all the day long,
And all the old ladies repaired to the smithy
  For fear that their Ticky-Tack-Toos would go wrong

The last few words of the song are not sung but spoken hurriedly as the convention that the song is ended. The Tailor looks up and catches sight of you. His eyes and his whole face light into a smile. The work is cast aside.

"Thon amon dieul! Welcome. Come inside and sit down. Herself has gone down the road for a piece, but she won't be long."

"What about the rest of the song?"

"There's no more of it, or if there is I no longer remember it. I learnt that many years ago from a great friend of mine – and it was a grand song. I used to know hundreds of songs, but when the voice goes you forget the songs as well."

"Well, what does 'Ticky-Tack-Too' mean?"

The Tailor glances up quickly before he answers.

"Yerra! it has no meaning at all. It is just a word. The poet's business was not to make sense but to make rhymes. Do you know that it was the poets who made all the words?"

Some other day he might explain – or he might leave the meaning of Ticky-Tack-Too to your imagination.

"But we are interrupting the work?"

"What 'interrupt'!" His eyes open wide with surprise and indignation. "The devil a bit 'interrupt'. It was only a bit of flannin jacket I was putting together. You don't see much of them nowadays. They are dying out like a lot of the good things. 'Bawneens' they used to call them, and damned good jackets they were. You'd be neither too hot nor too cold in them, and they were easily put on and taken off, and easily made. There's a great change come over the world since the days when every man wore a 'bawneen'. I remember well the day when no man living would be without a 'bawneen'."

The "bawneen" is cast aside, and the pipe is filled and lighted. Better, much better, to be talking of "bawneens" and the old days than making them.

"There's no dress nowadays looks half so well on a man as the dress they used to wear in those days. They would wear knee-breeches of corduroy, a vest of cashmere, a swallow-tailed body coat, a 'bawneen', a pair of low shoes and sheep-grey stockings. It was the biggest pity you ever saw to do away with them.

"But the clothes they wore in those days," he continues, between puffs, "were the devil to work, and well I know it, for I

23

was at the trade myself. Frieze, corduroy, pilot cloth, broadcloth and moleskin. There was nothing for them then but something firm and strong. I tell you those were the boys for wearing your fingers.

"Everything was different in those days. There were none of the mills and the factories that there are now. In every parish there was a man called a clothier. When you would shear the sheep you would spin and card and warp so many pounds of wool for him, according to your family, and he would take it to the weaver and get it woven into flannin and frieze and bring the cloth back to you.

"The next piece of the business was called 'whipping the cat'. The tailor would come and he would take the door off the hinges and put straw under it and sit down on it and cut and sew the garments he was to make on it. He would be several days at the job, and he would go on to another house when he had made all the clothes for you. He would be a journeyman tailor. He would hear all the talk wherever he was, and that was how tailors came to have a name for being wise men, as they are.

"For shirts they would set so many gallons of flax-seed, according to family, on the first of April, and it would be fit to pull in August. When it was pulled it was bound in sheaves and left to dry, and when it was dry they would put it into a pool in the river for five days' steeping. After that it would be taken out and spread in swarves to dry again and then made into sheaves and stooks and afterwards pounded with 'thourgeens' and cloved with a fake called 'a cloving tongs', which was a curious piece of business which would separate the flax from the tow. Another part of the business for separating the tow from the flax was called 'walloping the hackle'.

"Then you would spin the flax into threads the damn same way that you would do wool. You'd warp the threads then on the warping tree before you sent it to the weaver with the tow for woof.

"The weaver had an old sort of a measure called a 'bandel'. It was two feet long, and he would charge five shillings a score of 'bandels' for the weaving.

"I remember myself to see the end of the 'bandel'. It was prohibited by law, and I was looking at it the first bloody time the old R.I.C. prohibited its use in the market-place of Kenmare. That would be about forty-eight years ago. Now it is all statute measure, yards and feet, whatever good that does them.

"What the weaver made was canvas, and it was a dirty yellow sort of colour when it came back from him. You would bleach that yourself by soaking it with ashes of timber and water and leaving it in the sun to make it white out.

24

"I tell you, those were the shirts you would have out of it then. I knew a man to be eighty-nine, and all the shirts he ever had were two such linen shirts for all his lifetime.

"The world is a very different place to what it was in my young days. Nobody in those days would get a pair of shoes till he'd go to Mass, and that would be when he was eleven years of age. If you wanted shoes you would have to go to the fair at Bantry or Macroom or Kenmare.

"There'd be a man there with two or three kitches of shoes. You'd select a pair of shoes from him, and if they fitted you you'd buy them. The biggest price that you would pay for the biggest pair would be ten shillings.

"There were no right and left shoes in those days. Both shoes would be the same. The one you'd have on the left leg today you'd put on the right leg tomorrow. Brogues they used to call them, and damn fine shoes they were. You'd have no corns and bunions in those, I tell you. Do you know the best cure in the world for the likes of those?" the seventh son of a seventh son asks then. "Walk barefoot through the bog and you won't know your feet when you have finished.

"I remember well to see the first pair of shoes with a right and left foot that was ever made. They were made by a man by the name of Carol Daly, and a mighty smart type of a fellow he was. He could do every trade. He could farm and make shoes and harness and play the fiddle. He could use both hands, but do you know that his head was too smart entirely for his hands? Though he could use both hands they were not enough. He had to use his feet as well to keep up with his head. I saw him myself write four papers all at the same time. Two with his hands and two with his feet. Thamwirrashimfaina! I tell you there were some smart fellows in the world in those days."

Chapter Four

The Tailor is a gentleman of leisure. He stays in bed each morning until "Sean the Post" arrives on his way up from the village, with whatever letters there may be, and the much more important local news he may have collected on his four miles journey from the village.

But, as the Tailor says, he gets paid for simply being alive, sleeping or waking, in the form of his ten shillings a week pension, and he will not get any more by getting up any earlier. The rest of the people can air the world for him and put it straight before he gets up.

Ansty is full of busyness. She gets up with the dawn, kindles the fire, makes tea, lets out the cow, and from this until evening is always on the go. Though the Tailor may view much of her activity with scorn, someone must do the work of the place. The soda bread must be baked, the clothes washed, turf and water have to be carried, the cow and the hens and the ducks have to be fed, and in between, so that there will be no idle moment, the floor must be swept and swept and swept.

"Did you ever know how dust came to be invented?" asks the Tailor, after he has been disturbed innumerable times. "Well, I'll tell you the reason. When God made women they straightaway got into mischief. You see, He forgot to give them any sort of brains, and it was too late to do anything about it then. So He had an idea. He invented dust so that they should be all day sweeping it from one end of the house to the other. But it wasn't a great success. They still manage to get into mischief."

The Tailor does, however, play a part in the ritual of Garrynapeaka beyond that of critic. He tends the fire and cooks the dinner. He digs the potatoes and washes them and boils them. He prepares the meat. Then he tends and fills the lamps. Each day he has a round of duties and each day of the week there is some extra duty, particular to the day, added to his none too onerous burden.

On Wednesdays he "makes the churn", which is strenuous work for even a strong man. The churn is an old-fashioned dash churn, seldom seen nowadays, and the churn is "made" by working a plunger up and down in it until the cream "cracks" and the butter forms.

Sitting on Cornucopia, he twists his withered leg round the top of the little barrel and "slashes away", now and again pausing to sing a snatch of a song which has come into his mind. Then he salts the butter and that is Wednesday's labour finished.

Another day in the week you may come to the half-door and find him sitting before a tub and a basket, washing the eggs to fulfil the requirements of some Sale of Eggs Act. Of course, as soon as anyone appears the eggs are forgotten and all the evils of washing them remembered.

"Washing eggs! God blast it! Did you ever hear the like?" he says, as though he had been caught red-handed committing a crime. "As though people haven't eaten eggs for thousands of years without washing them until these politicians came along with their nonsensical notions. I tell you there's no face to it. One of these days the same politicians will come along and teach the hens how to lay them. It is a strange but a true thing, that the worse the Government the more Acts of Parliament they pass. I remember the days . . ." and so the Tailor's interest moves far away from his work on the eggs and his interest in them and he regains his seat on Cornucopia.

A shadow falls across the half-door.

"Thon amon dieul! I suppose you're tired," says the voice of Ansty with bitter sarcasm, "or the box in the corner was getting cold without your backside on top of it and the eggs can wait."

"By the mockstick of war!" replies the Tailor, "you'd think to listen to you that the whole country was crying out for eggs, and you were the only one who had them. They can wait till tomorrow," he adds with decision. "There'll likely enough be another Act of Parliament passed today whereby you'll be transported for washing eggs at all." And that day's labour is ended, at least, to the Tailor's satisfaction.

Each day has its round of general and particular duties, but the culmination of the week, the Tailor's most strenuous day, is Saturday.

The midday meal is finished. The Tailor has fed the cat and the dog. He has replaced the black hat upon his head and turned to the fire and is busy in the effort of getting his pipe to draw.

Ansty asks, "Have you cleaned the knives and the forks yet? Are you going to sit there for the rest of the day without stirring?"

"Maybe I will," answers the Tailor placidly between the puffs and the pulls. "I'm beginning to get a liking for the seat."

Ansty whirls out in disgust to attend to ducks or hens or the cow, and the Tailor continues to puff and to pull.

Soon, however, Ansty returns to the charge.

"Knives and forks! Knives and forks!" snorts the Tailor after listening to her for a moment. "Is the Pope coming to tea or what the hell ails you with your 'knives and forks'?"

About three o'clock he stirs himself and does get the box of knives and forks. There are about a dozen of each. They have never been used and are never likely to be used. They are of the company of the many dishes on the dresser and the many tins on "the clevy". They are ciphers in the life of Garrynapeaka, meaning nothing in themselves, as the noughts in a million, but just as important.

Out of Cornucopia the Tailor produces a knifeboard, some brick-dust and a polishing rag, and with much puffing and blowing he polishes them. The man who made them originally used far less effort in the making of them than the Tailor does in the needless cleaning of them.

Having by now got the flavour of stirring himself, he proceeds to his weekly shave. He takes water, out of the kettle, which Ansty always wants for some other purpose. Out of Cornucopia again comes a small mirror and a shaving-brush and razor. The razor is one given to him forty years ago by a friend in the old Royal Irish Constabulary. For forty years it was neither ground nor set, and was used for many purposes other than shaving. Shaving with it must have been either a magical process or a form of hell.

But those days are over. A friend took it over to London and had it ground and set in St James's Street. After the first shave with it the Tailor said that his face did not know the rest of his body and they had to be introduced to each other again. At last the shaving is finished. Life is arduous.

This is the one occasion in the week when he really feels in need of the refreshment of a cup of tea, and he puts the kettle hanging on the fire as soon as the shaving is finished. During the rest of the week he is indifferent to it. It is Ansty who hangs the kettle and is always ready for tea.

Down comes a contraption from the settle. It is a collapsible table with a hanging leg. One end rests on the settle and the other is supported by the swinging leg. It is just the right height for the Tailor seated on Cornucopia and the wrong height for anyone sitting on a chair. The Tailor is proud of this and enjoys your interest.

"What is it? Yerra, manalive!" he says, giving it a resounding thump, "that's a table. You've never seen the likes of that before I'll bet for a wager, yet that has been in this world for the past six hundred years, and you'd get a better meal off that than off any table de hote in the world."

"Have a cup?" asks Ansty, with a lively interest.

"Will 'oo have 'colouring'?" she asks then.

"Colouring" is Ansty's term for milk. She will present you with a really excellent cup of tea, far better than you will get in most hotels. The Tailor will ask you to have a cut of soda cake, or he will toast a slice of baker's bread for you. Ansty will ask you to have a boiled egg.

The Tailor will abide by your decision. Ansty will continue to persuade you, until a minor war breaks out between them and you, and the tea, and Ansty's hostess manners are all forgotten as they wrangle together. Suddenly the war ends as it started. Ansty hears someone passing and in the middle of a sentence leaps up, "Hould!" and rushes to the half-door to see who is passing, for all who pass must stand her scrutiny.

If they come into the yard she will speak to them over the half-door and you may hear your hostess in another manner.

"Have a 'heat of the tea'?" she invites.

The answer is always a refusal from those who know her.

"Scratch your bottom, then," is her answer, and she returns to the table to pick at a piece of bread like a bird.

Another duty of the day in which the Tailor is involved is that of winding the clock. Each evening, at about the same time, Ansty will break in upon his talk.

"Did you wind the clock?"

"I did not," replies the Tailor automatically.

"Better do it and then talk."

The cardboard box in the middle of "the clevy" is opened and a stout alarm-clock is taken out. It is given exactly the same number of turns of the key each night and replaced in the box and the lid of the box closed until the same performance the following evening. It is never consulted. No attention is paid to see whether it is right or wrong. The Tailor has some sort of a notion that it is a day wrong, but he is not sure whether it is a day fast or a day late. He is not interested in clock time.

"The best clock any man ever had is his belly. That tells him when it is time to eat. And when there is no one sitting by the fireside, then it's time to go to bed. And the time to get up is when you are tired of being in bed."

The Tailor is not interested in the clock. Ansty cannot read it. You wonder sometimes if maybe this clock, so carefully guarded in "the clevy" in Garrynapeaka, has more than ordinary importance, and if it may not be the clock of the universe, and if Ansty forgot to remind the Tailor to wind it, tomorrow the sun might fail to rise.

Along with the clock, each evening the Tailor has to be reminded to close and secure the outhouses. Ansty will wait, with malice aforethought, for an opportune moment to prick the bubble of his eloquence and rouse him to a sense of forgotten duty.

On one such occasion, his pipe drawing well, he was retailing the history of a former local resident, a General Gatacre, whose chief claim to fame, in the Tailor's estimation, was the fact that he once shot and ate one of the swans on the lakes near by. He was sailing gaily into the subject, which held all sorts of possibility of extension. Ansty, leaning on her broom by the door, waited until he had almost reached the climax of his story. Then her voice broke in.

"Go out and shut up the ducks," she commanded, "and close the fowls' house, and fasten the Room's window, and settle the door of the stall, and . . . you-can-come-in-and-sit-on-your-backside-for-the-rest-of-the-evening-and-talk-about . . . General Gatacre!"

The scorn with which she said "General Gatacre", as though the Tailor was far beyond his depth, defeated the Tailor utterly. He went out and did her bidding, and no one ever heard the end of the story of General Gatacre and the swan.

A duty which the Tailor does treat with respect is that of "standing to the cow". This consists of watching every movement of the black cow, exhorting it, checking it, shouting at it, getting Carlo to bark at it, building impregnable barriers between it and the oats and the cabbage and the potatoes.

In Ansty's scheme of things this cow comes first, and it is capable of every form of devilment that ever flickered through a cow's mind. If it is not guarded, it is liable to every misfortune that can possibly happen to a cow. Ansty, by the vehemence of her faith, seems to have won the Tailor to the same faith, and he grumbles only occasionally at this service to "the hub of the household". Only when at last the cow is shut up for the night in its warm and clean thatched stall does peace of any kind light upon Garrynapeaka.

The day ends with the last duty of all of the Tailor. At the end of the day, by the fireside, he and Ansty say the Rosary together in Irish. All the differences of the day are ended and forgotten, and the meaningless curses and the quarrels of habit and the rough, unvarnished words are solved, and banished with the prayers of the Rosary.

Chapter Five

The weather and the day's news had been discussed and dismissed.

"I was telling you the other day," started the Tailor, "of the way they had in the old days for managing clothes. But the world has changed a lot since then and a lot of the things they did and the ways they had have gone like the snow on Mangerton last year.

"Have you ever seen Mangerton mountain? It is one of the highest mountains in Kerry, and I know it well. You may be sure that I do, for I was born and reared within sight of it.

"My father was a farmer of twenty-four 'collops', in the parish of Kilgarvin, in the county of Kerry, and I was born there in 1862. Maybe you have not heard tell of 'collops'. It's a knowledge that is dying out of the world.

"Well, collops was the old style of reckoning for land, before the people got too bloodyful smart and educated, and let the Government or anyone else do their thinking for them. A collop was the old count for the carrying power of land. The grazing of one cow or two yearling heifers or six sheep or twelve goats or six geese and a gander was one collop. The grazing for a horse was three collops.

"I tell you, that was a better style of reckoning than your acres and your yards. It told you the value of a farm, not the size of it. An acre might be an acre of rock, but you know where you are with a collop. There is a man over there on the other side of the valley has four thousand acres of land, and barely enough real land to graze four cows in the whole lot. But you would think he had a grand farm when you talk of acres. The devil be from me! but the people in the old days had sense.

"There were thirteen of us in family, and I was the seventh son of my father, who was the seventh son of his father, so that the natural strain of a doctor is in me. I don't mean one of those galoots who have the title of being doctor but have no knowledge, but the type of doctor who has the knowledge within him and to hell with the title. Because a man has read a book does not mean that he is a wise man. There is too much learning in books nowadays, and too little learning in the head.

31

"We lived hard in those days. There was no tea and no bread and no sugar. I remember the first tea that came and how they made it. Some man who had been into Cork brought tea home as a great wonder, and had all the talk of what it would do. Well, his wife made a hand of it, and the way she had was to boil it and to strain off the water, and they fell to, eating the leaves as though it was cabbage. I saw that happen with my two eyes, as sure as there's a tail on a cat.

"We lived hard and we lived on the product of the land, on oatmeal, potatoes and milk. Probably we would kill an old cow or a couple of goats for Christmas, and that was all the meat we had for the year.

"When spring would come there would be as much potatoes as would do us until May. They usen't to set potatoes until July, and it is how they used to set them was to graff the scalp off the land with mattocks, and then when that dried, they burned it and shook the ashes on the ground. That was the manure they had.

"Then they would turn that into ridges with spades, for they had no ploughs, and they set the seed in the ground then and earthed it. They had fine potatoes called Black Minions. There are no such potatoes nowadays.

"It was in 1881 that the Champions first came to Ireland from Scotland, after the failure of 1880. They were allotted by the Board of Guardians. The law was that you would get so many hundred according to your valuation, and they should be paid for out of the poor rate. Poor people that had no land, but were workmen to farmers, would get two hundred by getting two securities.

"There was a man by the name of Dan Gill, who lived in Fussa. He had his two securities got and signed, and he went to Kenmare for three days, and it was failing him to get his potatoes because all the world was there. On the third day he got to the door of the court-house, after a struggle, to where the committee was, and he made application to them.

" 'You gentlemen before me are selected for the upkeep of the county and the welfare of the people, and I hope that you are conscientious men and do not make a zig-zag of your conscience, and that you understand the difference between God and Tom Bell (who is the devil's father), and that you will deal fairly with me, who am an old man, seventy-two years of age, and this is my third day walking twelve miles, six miles in and six miles out.'

"I took great admiration for this when I heard it. It was as fine and as good an oration as ever I heard.

"But to get back to the way we had of living in my young days. Before the potatoes would be ripe they would cut the corn.

They would burn the top of the sheaf of oats, and that would harden the oats for the quern, for the quern was how they used to grind the oats.

"The quern was a fake made with two flat stones, one on top of the other. You would put the oats between the two and turn the top one with a bit of a stick, and the oats between would be crushed. When the oats was ground in the quern, they would put the chaff and the shell into a tub, and put water on that, and leave it rest until tomorrow. That would lift all the chaff to the top. Tomorrow they'd throw that off, and what remained behind was 'flimmery'. They would put cold water on that for three days, and on the third night they would boil it, and it was the grand meal.

"They used to make a kind of bread with potatoes called 'Stampy'. They would grate the potatoes on a tin grater, and then squeeze them into a tub of water. From the water they would get the starch for the clothes. There was no such thing as a bastable in those days. The 'Stampy' was made on a breadtree, which was a kind of sloping board put before the fire to hold the bread, as you would make toast nowadays. 'Stampy' was usually only made for Christmas or November Night, unless you had a good supply of potatoes, when you might make it once a week.

"On the first of May the people would remove to the mountains, and make a bit of a house against a rock with sticks and scraws. They would carry their cattle, their milking cattle, with them, and milk them, and make butter and pack firkins, and send them to Cork by the carriers.

"When they were out of potatoes, they used to live on so many pints of blood out of the cow. First of all they would pull the rushes, and then pull the heart out of them and put it crosswise into a pot, and put the blood on to that. About halfways again they would put another crossing of rushes and then more blood, and then they would boil the blood until it was hard like a cake, and that was what they would have for food.

"They would make curds, too, of sour milk, and mix goats' milk through it. They would leave the whey run out of the door, and it would run out through the land. When November came, there would be a green stream of grass from the door, and they would measure this. By the length of this green stream the wealth of a man was measured. The man with the longest stream was the man who had the best times.

"They were hard ways of living then. Those were the days of the evictions and the Land League and the Coercion Acts. I remember, when Balfour's Coercion Act came out, a man described it this way:

You'll have to tell the hour that you were born,
And the way that you were got,
And the hour that you were made,
And how your mother met the man.

"That struck me as a very witty piece of business when I heard it.

"The people of this country were badly and unjustly treated, and that made the hardship of their lives the more. I don't blame the English people for this. It was the English Government, and you can't judge a people by its Government. I know that the English people had to suffer the same Government, and Governments are never made of the best of a people.

"But the English Government made a rod for their own backs. Did you know that the great Boer General, De Wet, who beat the English in the Boers' War, was of Irish descent? His father was an Irishman. I'll tell you the whole story.

"General De Wet's father was from Laune, west of Killarney. He was O'Connor, one of the O'Connor Balcarres, good, stout blocks of men. He was transported from Ireland to Algery on the west coast of Africa. They call it 'the white man's grave'. He was transported for smuggling tobacco, which was a custom they had in those days, and the devil a bit of harm was there in it. They did harm to no man.

"Well, enough, begod, he was landed in Algery, and he was put in a camp, and it wasn't agreeing with him at all. It wasn't long before he got away from them and went on the run. He faced up a mountain, and soon they had to give him up. He was too much for them, for he was a terrible loose type of a man, and mountains were nothing at all to him.

"Come the following morning, he faced down the other side of the mountain, and he hadn't gone very far at all when he came across some people, and they were all black. He had never seen the like before and they had never seen the like of him before; but being a decent, civil type of man he spoke to them.

"He had no English, but only the Irish, and to each man he met he said, 'Dia Dhuit' (Good day). That was his salute.

"By the hokey! when they saw him, never having seen the likes of him before, a white man, they thought that he was God, come down from Heaven, and they adored him and took him up and gave him the hell of a good time. He said to himself that this was better than the transportation camp, and he might as well die in June as July, so he anchored there.

"They called him De Wet, which was as near as they could get to the Irish, thinking it was his name. Anyway, after some time he got into a share of their ways, and they came to an understanding and he became a great man amongst them. Well, the devil a bit, but after a while longer he became intimate with one of the black women, and they got married, and they had a son, and that son was De Wet, General De Wet.

"I tell you that it was then that the English Government began to learn that they had only done themselves a great harm, when they thought that they were doing themselves a great good, by transporting O'Connor to Algery, thinking they had heard the last of him in 'the white man's grave'.

"They were hard times and they were difficult times, but there was plenty of fun. There were weddings and wakes and all sorts of amusements that the people made themselves.

"The people were very interested in dancing in those days, and there were dancing masters. They used to make a little hut, and you would carry a bag of turf tonight that would do the fire, and I would carry one tomorrow night. That was the payment. There were no such thing as 'sets'. There was only step-dancing, jigs and reels – no more.

"For music they had fiddles and flutes. There were no melodeons then. Sometimes there was not even fiddle and flute. Then they would dance to 'puss-music', music made by the mouth alone, without any instrument. I remember to see the first bagpipes made by some fellows, north in Ballyvourney, who made them from sheepskins and reeds and their own ingenuity, and a queer kind of music it sounded then.

"There was a dancing master in my time, by the name of Moriarty, who had an awkward block of a fellow to teach. It was failing Moriarty altogether to teach him how to batter, so, begod, he got a gad and put it on his left leg, and a sugan (hay rope) on the right, and he caught the ends of them in his two hands, and while the music was playing Moriarty sang this song.

> Rise upon Sugan,
> Sink upon Gad.
> Shuffle, me lad,
> Both Sugan and Gad.

"I tell you that he soon made a smart dancer of him.

"Hurley ball was the sport of my time. They made hurleys out of ash sticks, and a ball out of homespun thread from old stockings, covered with a leather covering. That was a terrible fierce game. There was no referee. There was no such thing as rules. It was a right murderers' game, but they were tough, strong men in those days, and they would think nothing at all of a blow which would kill a man nowadays.

"Tobacco was cheap, and porter was cheap, and whiskey was

cheap, and a man could get a deal of pleasure that way at little cost. The people, too, were a wittier, more airy people altogether. There was more talk, and good talk. There would never be a 'Scoruiocht' without some grand fun and songs and stories. The people had their own amusements. They had no need to seek other amusements.

"But that is all over now, like the fair of Athy, and the wise man is he who makes the best of what is, and remembers what was. I hear herself coming. I'd better look busy."

Chapter Six

The Tailor was perched on one of the big ivy and heather-covered rocks which dominate the acre of Garrynapeaka. He and Carlo had been set to mind the dairy herd. As long as the dairy herd kept well away from the cabbage and the oats, their job was simple, but at the first move towards these, the organization sprang into life.

The Tailor spoke to Carlo, and Carlo turned to the Tailor and barked and yelped until further orders. Never at the cow, but always at the Tailor. Carlo never approaches the cow. It is an original method, but it does work. Carlo acts as interpreter to the Tailor. He understands the Tailor's command and the dairy herd understands Carlo.

"It is a strange thing," the Tailor mused, when the noise had ceased, "but animals have their own language, and they can understand each other. The dog knows what I want, and he tells the cow; but we can't understand what they say to each other.

"Have you ever seen the raven?" he continued. "The raven is called the bird of knowledge. He builds his nest on the first of March and has young ones out for the first of April. The old people used to testify that if you got three of his eggs, and gave a drop out of each to a child before it was baptized, the child would come to know what the dog and all other animals say to each other.

"It could be the case, though I have never known it to happen myself; but the old people knew what they were talking about. They had a damn sight more wisdom than the people that is in the world today. They never spoke without reason.

"All the animals had the power of speech once. They could be understood, and we could understand them, and they could understand what we would be saying. Yerra, but that was a long time ago. Did you ever hear how they lost the speech? Well, I'll tell you.

"When the Jews were hunting our Saviour to crucify Him, He went, like I'd be west down the field and I'd be there and He spoke to me, and He told me shake oats on the ground.

"So I shook the seed, and it was ripe in the morning, and the Jews came in search trying to trick Him. And I was thrashing

37

the oats after cutting it, and they asked me, 'When was that oats set?' and I said to them, 'Probably about three months ago.'

"Well, so far no harm, and they were passing on with their trickery failed, but one of those things like a cockroach, which turns his tail up when he sees you – they call them 'the Devil's coachhorse' – stuck his head up out of the ground and said, 'Yesterday,' and the Jews came to know that our Saviour had passed that way.

"It was because of that that all the animals lost the speech, for they would tell everything.

"Ever since, every man, as soon as he sees this devil, and for the mean trick that he played on our Saviour, kills him with his thumb, by the sign of the Cross, saying, 'Seven of the worst of my sins upon you, and no sin of yours upon me.'

"A token of this is that the smell of the apple would be from him, and it is the smell of the apple of the garden of Eden. I tell you that the tokens of these things are there, though the people nowadays won't give in to them. The tokens are there, and the tokens are terrible. There is always a part of the apple of the garden of Eden stuck in a man's throat, and other tokens as well, if only we had the wisdom to understand them rightly.

"When the time came that all the animals were to be deprived of their speech, they could ask and hold three things. The cat asked for these three. That he would not be heard walking; that he would see by night as well as by day; that he would have the benefit of the housekeeper's neglect. I tell you that he was the smart fellow, and though he lost the speech he did pretty well for himself.

"I tell you, cats are the queer articles. You never know where you are with them. They seem to be different to every other class of animals. In the old days there were some foreign peoples who worshipped them, and it is not to be greatly wondered at, when you think of the intelligence of cats.

"I had a strange thing happened to myself years ago with cats. It was many, many years ago now. I had a calf to sell, and it was the time of the November fair in Macroom. I'd borrowed the loan of a crib and horse from a neighbour, and was ready to set off for the fair about one o'clock in the morning.

"Well, it came to one o'clock and I got up. I opened the door, and the night was so black that you would scarcely know which foot you were putting before you. I stirred up the fire and put some sticks under the kettle to make a cup of tea, and while it was boiling I went out to tackle up the horse. There was a mist coming down, so that I was wet enough already by the time that I had that job done.

"I made the tea, and while I was drinking it I thought what a foolish thing it was for me to be getting out of a warm bed and going into the cold, wet night and travelling for twenty-four miles through the night. But it had to be done, so I buttoned up a grand frieze coat I had, and off we set. The horse was as unwilling as myself for the road, and the two of us were ashamed to look each other in the face, knowing the class of fools we were. We travelled for hours and hours, and not much of the first hour had gone before I was wet through and through.

"As we drew nearer to the town I could see the lights in the farms by the roadside, where the people were getting up for the fair who had not to lose a night's sleep to get there. There was a regular procession now on the road of calves and cattle being driven into the fair, but it was still dark and the daylight was only just coming.

"Well, I took my place in the fair, and no one came to me and made me an offer for a long time. I thought that things were not going too well with me. Then a few asked me, but were offering only a poor price. I saw other cattle being driven away, and men I knew told me to sell, for it was a bad fair and prices were low. So at last I did sell, for the heart had gone out of me with the loss of sleep, and the long journey and the cold and the long waiting.

"I tell you that I was a miserable man, standing there with ne'er a bite to eat and wet to the skin, and with the prospect of the long journey home again, and the poor pay I had for my suffering. When I got the money I had something to eat and made a few purchases, and then I thought that if any man ever earned a drink it was me. So I met some friends and we had a few drinks together, and then parted and went our different ways.

"I let the horse go on at her own pace, with the reins hanging loose. The rain came down again, and the power of the drink soon wore off, and I wrapped myself up in my misery. With the sound and the swing of the crib and the creaking of the wheels and the darkness coming down again I fell asleep, as many a man does on the long way home from a winter's fair.

"Now and again someone passed me on the road, but I scarcely heard them at all. For miles and miles I went; now asleep, now awake, with all manner of queer notions running in my head, as does happen to a man when he is exhausted.

"As I was passing the graveyard of Inchigeela a cat put his head through the railings and said to me, 'Tell Balgeary that Balgury is dead.' I paid little heed to that, for my head was full of strange notions. I continued on my way. At last I reached home again, and untackled the horse and watered it and fed it, and then went into the house to change out of my wet clothes.

39

"Herself started on me straightaway. 'Tis wonderful the energy that does be in a woman's tongue and the blindness that can be in her eyes, for I was in no mood for talk.

" 'Well,' said she, 'what sort of a fair was it?'

" 'Ah! the same as all fairs,' said I.

" 'Did you get a good price?'

" 'I did not,' said I.

" 'Were there many at the fair?' she asked then.

" 'The usual number, I suppose. Did you expect me to count them?'

" 'Did ye hear any news while ye were in the town?'

"There was no end to her questions.

" 'Hold your tongue,' I said, 'and give me the tea.'

"I drank the tea and had a bite to eat and began to feel better. Still she kept on asking me questions.

" 'Glory me! Fancy going in all that way and hearing nothing at all,' she said, when I had no news for her. 'You might as well have stayed at home for all the good that you get out of a fair.'

"I got up from the table and sat by the fire and lit my pipe, but still she plagued me and pestered me with her questions. Had I seen this one? Was I speaking with that one? Was there any news of the other one?

"I suppose that the tea and the fire and the tobacco softened me. News and gossip are almost life to a woman, and she bore the hardness of our life as well, and I had brought her nothing home. Then I remembered the cat.

" 'The only thing that happened to me today,' I said, 'that has not happened on all fair days, was that when I was passing the graveyard of Inchigeela a cat stuck his head out of the railings.'

" 'Wisha! there is nothing strange in that,' she took me up.

" 'As I passed it called up to me, "Tell Balgeary that Balgury is dead." '

"At that, the cat, sitting before the fire, whipped round on me. 'The devil fire you!' said he, 'why didn't you tell me before? I'll be late for the funeral.' And with that and no more, he leapt over the half-door, and was gone like the wind, and from that day to this we have seen no sign of him."

The Tailor, being an honest man, enjoys his own jokes hugely, and his laughter spills down the rock on which he is perched.

" 'Tis a small thing would put a man in good-humour again, as the man said when he heard that his wife was dead, and he went out into the yard and saw the cock mounting the hen."

The sound of laughter has drawn Ansty. She comes round the corner. "Wisha! Listen to him! Full of the jokes and the laughing and the carry-on, and to hear him this morning in the bed, compla-a-ining and compla-a-ining and compla-a-ining!"

40

"Yerra! 'complain'. Mightn't a man spend his time complaining as well as any other way? A man has to find the faults in himself in order to improve. The devil a chance has anyone to sleep or do anything when you and 'Sean the Post' get together, screeching and bawling at each other and making more noise than all the war in Europe."

The Tailor is never nonplussed. He is equal to every occasion, be it man or event or notion. If the Pope walked in he would offer him a "heat of the tea", and most probably some advice, and he would forget him as soon as he walked out, unless, he appealed to him as a man. If an aeroplane landed on the road outside and the pilot offered him a trip he would go, as much to oblige the pilot, to be friendly, as for the experience.

All topics are open to discussion. He will, after a moment, explain some matter of which he has never heard before, and extend the subject with a story or an experience of his own, more or less apropos.

One day the beehive dwelling, a prehistoric relic in Kerry, was mentioned, and the Tailor was asked about it.

"Do you know the beehive dwelling up in the hills from Cahirdaniel, Tailor?"

"Cahirdaniel? You may be bloodyful sure that I do. Wasn't I born and bred within a few miles of it?" Every inch of Kerry is his province.

"But do you know the beehive dwelling there?"

"Yerra, manalive, who wouldn't know that?" There was just that slight hesitation that indicated that this was the first time that he had heard the mention of it.

"Tell us something about it then."

The pipe had to be lit and prodded into easy operation, and at last, after a thinking space, he was ready. There was a long draw and a spit.

"You couldn't have asked a better man," he started. Puff, puff and another light.

"The beehive dwelling at Cahirdaniel? I remember that being built as well as I remember today. It was built by a man by the name of Sullivan, who was a near neighbour of ours." Now he is getting into his stride.

"I tell you, he was the smart man. He was the best engineer that Ireland ever produced, and I knew him well. I was at school with him. That man had more ingenuity in his little finger than most people have in their whole bodies."

Now the pipe was drawing well, and the Tailor's imagination was running just as freely.

"He done contracts for building all over the place. Car-houses, and pigsties, and the neatest houses ever a man laid his

41

eyes upon. He built bridges and roads over bogs that hold well to this day."

"Well, why did he build this? It seems to be a useless sort of a place, surely."

"Wisha! that was nothing to him. He just built that in his idle time."

"But why did he build it? What is it for?"

"What for? Why, for no reason at all beyond the exercise of his own ingenuity. Things like that were like daisies in a bull's puss to him."

So much for archaeology.

On another occasion someone brought in a portable wireless set, and asked the Tailor if he would like to hear the news from London.

"I don't mind whether it is from London or China or Algery. It is all the same as long as it is news, and it will be good to hear how the folks are doing there."

The set was switched on. For fifteen minutes the Tailor listened to the suave announcer from the B.B.C. His eyes popped a little at first. He held the set in his hands, and there was a moment when he was either a little awed or afraid.

When the news was finished he gave his opinion. "That fellow knows his geography pretty well. He should get full marks. But I wonder if he could find his way on a misty night from Barlin to Lackabawn. Ask him, will you, if he has any news of the people in Tir-na-n-Og, or if he knows what is going to happen tomorrow."

That was the limit of his interest in it. He turned from it to some local matter of much more intimate importance.

The first time that he saw a typewriter he was impressed, and when its function was explained to him he wanted straightaway to write a letter. With the impression that great force writes the letter, he started. In the middle of the work, "Dan Bedam" walked in to redden his pipe.

"Dan Bedam's" work carries him often during the day on the road which runs past the Tailor's cottage, and he comes in many times to redden his pipe or to hand on a bit of news. . . . All his conversation starts with "Bedam", so the Tailor has christened him "Dan Bedam".

"Bedam, Tailor, what's that?"

"That's a typewriter, Dan. It's a patent for writing. It will write English and French and Irish and German, and big letters and small letters, and spell every word correctly, and it will do sums as well."

"Bedam," said Dan, taking off his hat and scratching his head. "I've never seen the likes of that before."

42

"Faith, but there are many wonders in this world that you have not seen yet, Dan."

"Bedam, but that's true for you, Tailor." The hat came off again, and Dan scratched again. "The man who made that must have been a mighty clever fellow," he decided.

"Yerra! What? 'Clever!' To make an ould machine? You're a cleverer fellow than he was yourself."

"Bedam, how could that be?" puzzled Dan, scratching harder.

"Thamwirrashimfaina! Do you know that the man who made this machine was married ten years, and he could not make one small lad, and you have made five of them yourself?"

"Bedam! that's true enough," said Dan, replacing his hat with a beam of self-satisfaction, and the two of them turned away from the typewriter, to discuss the more proximate matter of Johnny Con's new bull.

It was at the Astoria Cinema that the Tailor first saw the "talkies", though on the way down in the car, he did say, when the subject of the cinema was mentioned, that he had seen them over forty years ago in Cork.

"But you did not see the talking pictures, surely?"

"Wisha! Of course I did. Didn't I pay my money and see the whole bloody caboodle?"

"And the people in the pictures talked?"

"Why wouldn't they talk? I tell you that there was nothing they would not do for you. They would sing, run, dance. They would even have small lads for you."

It was a command performance. Four of us sat in the gallery. The manager was very obliging, and went in his car to bring the operator back from a fishing trip, for the afternoon was too fine, and the audience, until we arrived, did not exist at all.

The curtains were drawn across and the dynamo switched on.

"Thon amon dieul!" exclaimed the Tailor when he heard the hum of the dynamo. "Now the praties are boiling, and we won't be long."

We had a news reel, which included a horse race. This started in a rush, while the Tailor was in the act of lighting his pipe, and his attention was divided.

"The devil break your legs! What is all the hurry about? Haven't we the rest of the day to ourselves? Can't you hould while I light my pipe?"

But the pipe was forgotten in the excitement of the race, and the Tailor called out advice and abuse to the jockeys. After the news reel we had slides of local advertisements. The Tailor read each one and commented upon them all.

"Drink O'Leary's Lemonade."

"Who the hell wants to drink that stuff when he can get decent porter? That's one of the things that is ruining this country. It is thinning the people's blood till it is only like water and making their teeth fall out before their time."

A slide advertising a permanent wave baffled him. "You'll look your best in a Burke's Beauty Wave." He read that through twice, and was still puzzling over it when it was shot away and gave place to "Try O'Driscolls for Drugs".

"A decent, tidy slip of a man," approved the Tailor. "I knew his father well. He was near related to me. He got married to a girl by the name of MacCarthy, from the Dunmanway side. She had a farm of land of her own. But after they were married he was not long before he drank it out. Many's the piece of a night we spent together, and many's the half-gallon of porter we drank together in the old days. It was the drink that killed him in the latter end – God rest his soul – though some say it was the pneumony; but I know damn well that it was the drink."

The Tailor's reminiscences of the O'Driscolls were cut short by a reminder that "You can be sure of Sullivan's shirts".

"Sullivan's shirts! Pshaw! Do you know that that fellow is the biggest rogue that ever walked on two legs. Years ago I bought a calico shirt from him, and I paid dear for it, and it didn't last me more than a couple of months. God blast it! He ought to be in gaol. But his brother is the same. They were all a bad lot. Sullivan's shirts! Sullivan's shirts!"

The advertisement finished. They and their vaunted power had passed the Tailor by completely. He had ripped right through them to the man and the thing. The words were not hypnotics but stimulants to him in an entirely personal way.

We were not completely free from advertisement, however, for next we had a trailer for the coming week. "Coming next week! Yerra, you'd think it was in church that we were – bothering our heads about next week or next year. That's a queer way to be enjoying yourself. To hell with next week. Let's have this week first. We may be dead and buried by next week."

The big film started. It was a matrimonial tangle on a pleasure cruise. The Tailor enjoyed every moment of it, and explained every detail of it, and gave advice to every actor in it.

Very soon the hero and the heroine were engaged in a shy love scene.

"Hould her! Hould her! You'd think by the shaping of her that she did not like it, but I tell you that they are all that way in the beginning. It is a way they have of letting on that they don't like it, when all the time they like it as a donkey likes strawberries."

The hero disappointed the Tailor. He was altogether too shy and diffident, and the Tailor lost patience with him.

"Thon amon dieul! Man, if I was twenty years younger, I'd come up there and give you lessons."

The heroine was altogether too young and skittish for him. He transferred his affections to her mother. "A nice class of a woman, and I'll bet a wager that she has a bit of money. A man could do much worse than to marry the likes of her. He could knock a winter out of her comfortably."

The Hollywood beauties were a little too slim for him. "They are a merry lot of jolly cuppers, but they are half-starved. They should throw some food at them and fatten them up and make them comfortable. They need a basinful of stirabout and thick milk a few times a day, and then they would be all right."

Even the fat lady was not exactly to his taste. "A devil of a great pounder of a woman. She'd make a handy door for a car-house. She'd stifle you in the bed. People think that fat women are warm. I tell you that they are not. They make a damn great tunnel in the bed, and a man may as well be sleeping in a gully."

It ended at last. The lights went up.

"All over now, like the fair of Athy," was the Tailor's comment.

Like all good dramatic critics, we retired to the pub across the road, and the Tailor gave us his considered opinion about the whole performance. He admitted that there was a considerable improvement since his former visit to the cinema, forty years ago. "The speech is plainer, and the women are better-looking, except that they are a bit on the thin side; but how the hell did that fellow of the shirts, Sullivan, stick his nose in there? I'd like to go back to have a few words with him. Sullivan's shirts. Sullivan's shirts!"

He explained it all to "The Sheep" the following Sunday evening. "The Sheep" is somewhat older than the Tailor, and visits him regularly each Sunday evening from the next valley. He wears a stiff-fronted shirt and a hard hat which mounts to a point at the top, and must be the father of all hard hats, it is so ancient.

He sits on the settle and leans with his two hands folded on his stick. He seldom speaks beyond an encouraging grunt or a confirmatory echo to the Tailor's discourse. He happens to be one of the few people for whom the Tailor has neither affection nor respect. He is condemned for meanness, a fault which ranks very high in the Tailor's category of faults.

"Would you believe it, looking at that man and listening to him, that in his young days he read most of the books that were ever printed; yet he is so damned mean that he would not give you so much as his opinion of the weather!"

45

"The Sheep", the ancient bookworm, was impressed with the Tailor's description of his visit to the cinema. Even he was roused to comment on "Sullivan's shirts".

"Yes. Yes," he agreed, as though his life depended upon agreement, "I have heard tell of him—but," he added, lest he compromise himself any way, "I never wore one of his shirts. But maybe you are right, Tailor, maybe you are right. Such things could be," came as a token from guest to host.

He absorbed all the details and the explanations as a hungry man would devour food. His eyes and his ears were intently occupied. When the Tailor had finished he got up and gave forth the product of his mental digestion.

"It must have been something like that that the old people saw, when they saw funerals walking into the side of a mountain, I expect."

"Funerals! Funerals!" snorted the Tailor as soon as "The Sheep" was beyond the door. "Did you hear that for the height of cleverness, so that you would think that he was stupid, and he has as good as been to the pictures without it costing him a penny or without putting one leg before the other. The devil fire him and his – funerals!"

Chapter Seven

The rain was slashing down outside. All the Tailor's duties had been performed. Ansty had at last settled down and there was a merry fire on the hearth.

"Did you ever hear tell of a class of fellows called 'the cabogues'?" asked the Tailor, as the prelude to a story. "Well, I'll tell you a story about two of them, and what happened to them.

"In years gone by it was ever a custom of fellows from Castletown and Allihies and such-like places to go down to Limerick, to dig spuds for the farmers in the autumn. They were known as cabogues. They would start off on Saturday morning with a spade and a shirt, and go to Mallow that night, no matter what the distance. The following day, Sunday, after Mass, the farmers would be looking for the men for hiring.

"Well, there were two young recruits to the game. They would be about eighteen years of age, and it was their first time going on the expedition. They set out good and early, and that night they reached Mallow. They had never been in the likes of the town of Mallow before, and they knew no one there.

"They did not know where they would sleep that night, so they asked a man they met in the street, and he took them to a lodging-house and told them to anchor there. They had the supper, and when the time came for them to go to bed they were surprised where they were going, when the landlady showed them the way upstairs.

"This was a great wonder to them, for at that time in the country there was no upstairs nor loft to any house. Just a room here and another one off it, all on the level.

"There were two beds in the room. They were told to sleep there, but one bed would do them, they said, as they always slept together.

"Well, begod, the landlady walked down from them, and as soon as she was gone they set to, and looked round the room and examined everything in it, for it was all strange to them. There was in it all manner of things, the like of which they had never set eyes on before. They came to the beds. They examined the fine linen on them and the frames of them. Then one of them looked underneath and he found a pot.

" 'That's a queer article,' said he, pulling it out.

" 'It is,' said the other fellow, pulling out the pot from under the other bed, and studying it. 'What can they be for, I wonder?'

" 'The devil alone knows,' said his companion. 'Could they be the tea-cups of Finn MacCool?'

" 'Not at all,' said the other fellow, who did not want to appear ignorant. 'I'll tell you what they are. They are night-caps, of course.'

"So they put on their night-caps and into bed with them, and they slept very comfortably entirely. At that time a four-horse coach left Mallow for Newcastle West at six o'clock in the morning. They used to call it a Jingle by the noise of the bells on the harness.

"Well, the devil a bit but the following morning my two jolly cuppers were wakened by the noise of the Jingle under the window, and they wondered what it could be. Out of the bed with them, and they stuck their heads outside the window to solve the mystery.

"The night-caps fell off into the street below and broke with the hell of a noise, which frightened the horses, and away with the Jingle and the grooms chasing it and shouting, and the passengers screeching, and everybody in Mallow thinking, with all the noise and clatter, that surely the last day had come. But it was all due to two cabogues who did not know the difference between a pot and a night-cap.

"But that was not the end of the expedition. The two cabogues were hired in Mallow that day, and went out to the potato digging. They earned good money, and at last the season was over, and they had to be taking the road for home again.

"Their route took them by way of Tipperary, and as they were passing along a road they came to a notice which said that for the payment of half a crown anybody could look at the Ratschilds' money.

"Now the Ratschilds were the richest people in the whole world, and the head of them lived in Tipperary. (I'll tell you afterwards how they came to get the money and the name.) It was a custom of the head of them to let people see the wonder of money that they had, and to charge them for the sight of it, as the notice said.

"Said one cabogue to the other when they had the notice read, 'I'm thinking that I'll take a look at that.'

" 'Thamwirrashimfaina!' said the other to him, 'have you gone clean mad, to be paying half a crown to see another man's money? Have sense, man.'

" 'I have sense enough,' replied the other. 'It is seldom that

48

the chance will come our way to be able to see such a wealth of money as the Ratschilds' money.'

"'Go your way, then,' said the sensible fellow, sitting on the bank of the road and lighting his pipe. 'I will wait here for you.'

"So, in with the first cabogue to the house, and he knocked on the door. The head of the Ratschilds opened it to him.

"'Good day,' said the cabogue. 'I have come to see your money.'

"'That will cost you half a crown,' said the Ratschild.

"So my jolly cupper handed him the half a crown, and the head of the Ratschilds took him into the room where the money was. In one corner was a heap of gold. In another a heap of silver, and in another a heap of coppers. The cabogue looked at it in wonder, for never before had he seen so much money in one place.

"'Well,' said the Ratschild, after a few moments, 'aren't you the foolish man to be paying me half a crown to look at my money?'

"'Yerra, not at all,' replied the cabogue. 'Doesn't the sight of it give me as much pleasure as it does you?'

"'True for you,' replied the Ratschild, scratching his chin. 'I suppose that it does. You are a smarter fellow than I thought,' he went on, 'for you have taught me, the richest man in the world, a lesson.'

"'Ah! say no more about it,' said the cabogue.

"'No,' answered the head of the Ratschilds, 'you deserve a reward. Help yourself.'

"So the cabogue took up a fistful of gold and a fistful of silver, and out with him to the other fellow outside, who was still smoking his pipe.

"'Now,' said he, showing him the money, 'am I the foolish fellow or are you?'

"'The devil fire you,' said the other fellow, 'you are a smarter fellow than I thought.'

"'That is exactly what the Ratschild said to me,' said the fellow with the money, 'but he paid me for the lesson I taught him, but we will say no more about it.'

"They went on their way and they came to a pub, and they went in and called for two half-gallons of porter, and drove the devil of a spree together.

"I suppose that you have heard of the Ratschilds and how they are the richest family in the world; but I bet for a wager you don't know how they came to be so wealthy, and how they came by the name.

"They started in Cork. Ratschild isn't their right name at all. They are really Kellihers, but they changed that. They used to be house painters in the beginning, and one day one of the brothers was painting a house, and he was on the scaffold having a smoke for himself, when he saw a rat come out of a hole, and it had a sovereign in its mouth.

"Rats are curious animals. They are very fond of collecting bright things and carrying them away to their nests. Well, this man by the name of Kelliher, went on quietly smoking and thinking to himself that house painting was a poor sort of life, and how he wished he had enough money to start some other kind of business, when he saw the rat come out again, and it had another sovereign. It placed this with the other and went back.

"Kelliher went on smoking and did nothing to frighten the rat, and the rat went on carrying out sovereigns and making a pile of them. When at last he had made a good pile, Kelliher threw his paint-brush at it, and came down from the scaffold, and collected up the pile of sovereigns and counted them, and found that he had come into the way of being a rich man.

"That was the beginning of the Ratschilds. They discontinued the house-painting business and started a bank and soon were in a mighty way of business, and, because they had made their beginning from the money the rat had collected, they were ever afterwards called the Ratschilds, and the devil blast the lie it is.

"It is a queer thing the way fortunes are made, and how men come to be rich. It is seldom by hard work. Hard work chiefly kills a man. Did you ever hear the story of Laddin, and the curious thing that Laddin found, and the wonders that it would do?

"It all happened in Paris, which is the capital of France, except sor.• part of it which happened in a big meadow in South Africa. It happened a long time ago, for I heard it told by an old man when I was a boy, and he was a young man when it happened.

"One day there was a party of young fellows playing a game of handball in the main street of the city of Paris. There was one fellow amongst them whose name was Laddin, and whose father was a tailor who was dead.

"A man, by the name of Musapha, came up to this young fellow and asked him was he Laddin.

" 'Yes,' said he, 'the devil a wonder but I'd be Laddin. Wasn't I christened Laddin?'

" 'Well,' said Musapha, 'will you come for a walk?'

" 'I will,' said Laddin, 'but I would like to tell my mother first.'

" 'Ah! To hell with your mother!' said Musapha then, 'we won't be long away.'

" 'All right then,' consented Laddin.

"They struck out of the town about three miles at their ease, and they went into the corner of a wood. Laddin was getting scared, but at the same time he took it softly and made the best of it. There was a small patch at the end of the wood where there was no grass growing, and Musapha put a ring on Laddin's small finger and told him to work with that finger in the ground.

"So Laddin did as he was told, and the devil a bit but he had only little done, when the place opened, and down he went with the devil's own landing, and the place overhead closed.

" 'By the hokey!' said Laddin then, 'I'm in the hell of a fix.'

"He shouted and called away, but no one answered him, and he was thinking that he would never again get up. But soon he came to steps, and trying to climb up them, and in the act of climbing up them in the dark, for there was ne'er a splink of light, he struck the ring against the steps and the ring asked what did he want.

" 'Yerra, manalive,' said Laddin, 'what do you think I'd want but to get out of this place. Do you think that I am screeching for the fun of the thing?'

"The ring told him to go to a crevice in the cave and there he would find a lamp, and to bring the lamp with him.

" 'Talk sense, man,' said Laddin. 'How can I find a lamp in a crevice when I cannot see my own hand?'

"The ring then told him to calm himself and to make search. Well, he made search, thinking that he might as well do that as any other thing, and he found the lamp. When he was above ground again Musapha was there, and Laddin gave him a relement.

" 'The devil break your legs, didn't you hear me calling to you? It is a queer kind of fun to watch me fall into a bog hole and give me no help.'

"When Laddin had finished, Musapha told him to keep the lamp carefully, and anything he wanted it would do him, to put his thumb into his mouth, and to chew it and then tell the lamp, and the lamp would tell him what to do.

"He thanked Musapha and told him that he was grateful to him, but Musapha said, 'Not at all. Damn it, it was nothing entirely.'

"They walked the three miles back into the city, and there they parted and Laddin went home. His mother asked him where he had been, and why he was late for the tea, but he told her nothing at all. He went to bed after he had something to eat, for he was tired after the day's expedition, and he took the lamp with him and put it in a safe place under the bed.

"When he got up the following morning his mother said to him that there was nothing for the breakfast, for they were very poor. He thought of what Musapha had told him, and he went to the room above again and took out the lamp from under the bed, and put his thumb in his mouth and chewed it and told the lamp the trouble.

"The lamp talked and told him, 'You make chinaware and take it out and sell it.' So he took the lamp down over a table and struck it and told it to make chinaware. Down came a cup and saucer of chinaware. It was the prettiest piece of business ever a man did see. He made a dozen of each and took them out to the neighbours and sold them, and then they had the fine breakfast.

"After they had the breakfast finished he made some more, and put them in the window. The news got around, and the world got surprised, and the people came in troops, buying, and he selling, and all the time the grand ware was rattling on to the table as fast as he could sell it. Then he told it to make dishes and so on, and the lamp went obstreperous and there was no stopping it at all, and the chinaware was pouring over the room and out into the street, and he came up to make a terrible big fortune.

"After a while the lamp got tired and stopped, and Laddin himself took a rest and got married. When he was married he no longer had time for the hardware business, so he put the lamp under the bed again, where only he and his wife slept, and he told no one.

"One day he went out for a walk by himself, and some fellow in the city, who had been watching his movements, bought fine, grand, new lamps, and went round the houses calling, 'New lamps for old!' He came to Laddin's house and walked in to his wife, and asked her for any old lamp she might have, and he would give her a fine new lamp for it.

"She remembered that one day when she was dusting and poking about she had come across the old lamp under the bed and, with the height of madness, she went upstairs and brought down the old lamp and gave it to him. He fulfilled his part of the bargain and then skedooed off. He asked the lamp where they should go, and the lamp told him to South Africa, so there they spent the night.

"When Laddin came home from his walk, his wife told him of her bit of business, and showed him the grand new lamp and asked him if it was not the fine bargain.

" 'Thon amon dieul!' exclaimed Laddin, 'we are done for ever.'

" 'But, sure,' said she, 'wasn't it thrown idle?'

" 'Idle me foot! That's the worst of the senselessness and the interference of women! If you would but attend to the business of the house, and not the things which do not concern you, all would have been well. We are ruined and disgraced.'

"He would eat no dinner. Away with him saying that he would travel the world for ever till he found the man who had stolen the lamp; and then it would go hard with him. So he travelled for four days and for four nights, and the fourth night he slept under a hedge.

"When he woke he went to a stream to wash his face, and in the act of taking up water to his face he struck the ring upon a rock and the ring asked him what ailed him, and whyfor was he travelling the world.

"'What ails me? Why am I travelling the world? Aren't those foolish questions! What the devil do you think ails me? Do you think that I am travelling the world for the good of my health?'

"'Aisy now, aisy,' said the ring. 'I'll tell you all that you want to know if you but listen.'

"Then the ring told him that the man who had stolen his lamp was in the middle of a big meadow in South Africa, and was in the act of enjoying the finest breakfast ever a man did see, provided by the power of the lamp.

"At that Laddin said that himself should go to South Africa, and with that he set off, and he never stopped until he got there, and he found the man just finishing his breakfast and the lamp beside him. He had a few words with him and took the lamp from him and by the power of it he changed the man into a stone statue so that he should steal no more lamps. When he had this done he sat down and finished the breakfast, for there were lashings of the finest food.

"Then he felt better and returned to Paris with the lamp, leaving the man in the field to this day. He started again in the hardware business, but no longer sought his conjugal rights with his wife, but left well alone and lived happily."

Chapter Eight

"I was just thinking," said the Tailor amidst the engrossment of poking and prodding his pipe, "before you came in—"

"Pity you haven't something better to do," interrupted Ansty, "but be poking your old pipe and shm-o-o-king like a chimney and – thinking, all the day. 'I was just thinking,' says he, as though he had a great wonder done," she repeats venomously.

"Hould your whist, woman! I was not talking to you.... What started it was a woman who walked down the road the other day while I was standing to the cow. When she saw the cow, I declare to God didn't she ask me if it was a bull or a cow—"

"A bull or a cow! Glory be! Asked if it was a bull or a cow!" echoes the chorus.

"—and she wasn't a young woman either, and she was married by the ring on her finger—"

"Married – and asked 'Was it a bull or a cow?'" Ansty is stunned with amazement. The joke seems too absurd even for her. "Hould, you divil!" she hurls at the Tailor to check his extravagance. "It passes all belief."

"—and she had been drinking milk all her life – and, manalive! she didn't know the difference between a bull and a cow."

"Married and didn't know the difference between a bull and a cow," Ansty muses, as though the Tailor's reiteration of the fact has weaned her from her former incredulity. Once or twice she repeats the statement until it is completely absorbed. Then she starts again.

"Gon rahid!" (Gan raht ... May you have no luck.) "That was the queer kind of marriage. What was she married to? They must have had the strange carry-on. Didn't know the difference between a bull and a cow, and married!" Whatever goes on in Ansty's imagination gives her great glee, to judge by her chuckles. Still repeating the phrase, "Didn't know the difference between a bull and a cow", and still chuckling away to herself she goes out to the ducks and the hens.

The Tailor takes up from the interruption.

"She didn't know a bull from a cow. That is what started me

thinking. Thon amon dieul! but I swear that the world's gone to alabastery. It's queerer it's getting every day. Would you believe it that there are people nowadays who don't know wheat from barley and yet eat bread, and can't tell the difference between a cock and a hen and eat eggs like this one, and her – 'Is it a cow or a bull?'

"It's a strange sign of the times. No wonder that the world be as it is. The more education they have the less they know. The people in the old days had no education or only very little, but they were a deal smarter and wiser than the people that is in the world today. They knew the world they lived in and didn't go round like fools, asking, 'Is that a bull or a cow?' The people that is going now don't know that or anything else.

"It puzzles me what the people nowadays do learn, and what they have in their heads. We all know that they can read and write. We can all do that, and a share of the old people could do that, too. But the men haven't the bone or the strength to do much, and the women can neither cook nor breed, nor do any damn thing but cackle like hens, and make themselves look uglier every day.

"There's millions of pounds of good money spent on education, and what's the result? They don't know the difference between a bull and a cow. By the mockstick of war! it's no wonder that there is trouble in the world; and that there will be until the people get a bit of sense and a bit less education, and do a bit of thinking for themselves instead of getting everything ready-made out of books.

"For learning is like a suit of clothes. The cloth is there, but it has to be cut to the measure of every man. What fits me won't fit you, and what fits you won't fit me. Then, when the suit is made, it is mine or it's yours. The same suit won't fit the two of us. It's the same with education. The knowledge is there, like the cloth. It is there for every man. It isn't in books, but in living. We have to cut and measure and sew to suit ourselves. We have to do our own thinking.

"There have been all classes of people in here with me at different times. People who write books. People who teach in colleges and universities and such-like. But do you know, the airiest, wittiest men that ever walked into me were the men who walked the roads; men such as Jerry of the Sack, Tom Malone and Jerry Cokely – God rest his soul.

"They were the men who had the talk and the idees and the imagination. It was they who saw the world and lived in it, and were the smart and clever fellows. I'd as soon see one of those cross my doorstep as anyone, for they are always conversible, intelligent men, though people think them queer because they

55

had their own way of living, and lived away without doing any man harm.

"It's a mystery to me that, with all this education and talk of education, it should make so many stupid people, and such people poor for living and poor in living. Thamwirrashimfaina! if a man does not use his own eyes and ears and mouth and intelligence, he may as well be dead. There's no man living can't see a new wonder every day of his life, if he keeps his eyes open and wants to see. There's no man who cannot learn every hour of the day, and be a wiser man at the end of each day until the day he dies.

"I remember years ago there was a priest in Adrigoole preached a sermon on miracles. After the sermon he was talking to a man by the name of Murphy, Tim Murphy, a half gommerish sort of a fellow.

" 'Well, Tim,' said the priest to him, 'did you enjoy the sermon today?'

" 'I did, Father,' replied Tim. 'It was a damn fine sermon entirely.'

" 'Did you understand it?' asked the priest then.

" 'I did, Father. Every bloody word of it but one.'

" 'Oh!' said the priest. 'What word was it that you did not understand?'

" 'Miracle, Father. I didn't understand the meaning of the word "miracle" – nor I don't yet!'

"The people nowadays are like Tim Murphy. They spend years at schools and colleges, and then sit still for the rest of their lives like dummies. They know nothing, and you might as well be talking to a bush at the side of the road as talking to them, for all the good you'd get out of them. Leave me alone with them. They've gone obstropelous.

"I have known men of my time, with even less education than I had myself, who went to America and made big positions for themselves, and came to be famous men. Weren't there several presidents of America who were Irishmen? But the people nowadays, with all their education, won't do that. They can't do that. They will scarcely breathe for themselves unless they get a grant from the Government.

"I remember, years ago, seeing a kind of a circus where they had a play, and all the actors were dolls. They moved and danced and walked, but all that was done with threads tied to them, and there was a fellow above who pulled the threads. That is what the people that is going nowadays seem like – dolls who won't move until the threads are pulled, and who won't speak unless the words are put into their mouths.

"Things have taken a queer turn. We used to be mad for education in the old days. We used to think that if we could read and write we were the wonder of the world, and there was nothing we could not do. All we needed was knowledge. Well, the people have knowledge. Much more than there was in the old days, but they have ended up like dolls.

"But there is a deal of difference between the knowledge you get out of a book and the wisdom that comes into your own head by living and by using yourself, and that is the difference between the old days and the present times."

There are footsteps outside. Ansty comes in and puts down a pail of water with a clatter.

"Wisha! a married woman who didn't know the difference between a bull and a cow! No wonder the world is queer."

There is the usual few minutes' disturbance of dust, atmosphere and continuity which Ansty's presence produces, and the Tailor fills the time in packing his pipe. Ansty disappears again on one of her thousand excursions of the day. The Tailor takes up the broken thread of talk once more.

"In my time there was no national school. Only the 'fodeen', the hedge school. Each pupil would pay two or three pence each week, and the master would come home with you tonight and with me tomorrow, and have his supper and bed and breakfast as part of the payment. Some of them were learned men, right scholars. Others of them could read, but were not so good at writing. Some were good at poetry, and some were good at geography.

"I was seven years of age when I went to school, and to a fodeen school. The lessons were like this. You would spell and read so much of a book. Then you would do parsing. 'The' a definite article. Parsing was bloody awkward, I can tell you. It was a work of the devil himself. I was never much good at it.

"You would learn chapters of geography at home, and you would have two cards of arithmetic along with that. You would learn to write by drawing pot-hooks and hangers, until you were an expert at the game. The writing of the old people was a damned sight plainer and better-looking than the writing of the people in the world today, and that was the reason of it.

"That would be from Monday until Thursday. Friday would be repetition day, when you went through all that you had learned during the week, to see that you had it well stuck into your skull.

"For geography there would be a big map of the world or a globe, and the teacher would call out names of places and you'd find them on the map. There was hardly a fellow went to school in those days who would not be able to travel the world, they knew it so bloody well on the map, and many of them did.

"At the finish of the day you would say the Rosary and go home.

The worst scholar of the day would be punished. It was a queer kind of punishment. He would have to carry home with him the skull of an old horse or donkey and carry it back the next morning. There was another custom they had in those days too. If they built a new house anywhere, they would always try to bury the skull of an old horse in the kitchen floor. I have often wondered why this was, but I have never been able to discover.

"Most of the scholars would stay only two or three years. Education was a new thing in those days, and there was plenty of work to be done. But they seem to have learned more in that time than they do with all the years they have now.

"At the time of the big emigration to America, I saw grown men, maybe twenty-three or twenty-four years of age, who were thinking of going to America going back to school to better their education. There were thirty or forty such men going with me to school when I was going.

"All the schooling was in English. There wasn't a syllable of Irish. It was against the law, and you would be beat if you used it. But the people had the Irish, and good Irish too, and they spoke it amongst themselves. Now the world has changed round, and you are paid to learn it and few people have it. It's a queer state of affairs.

"You'd start with slates and slate pencils for writing and arithmetic. They were a handy idea, for you could wipe away what you had written and you could make a devil of a noise with the pencil on the slate. There would be no copy-book for you until you had been about a year at school.

"Well, that was my education. I learned to read and write and do arithmetic, and to know the world, and to think for myself, and to know the difference between a bull and a cow. I left school when I was thirteen years of age, and I was bound to a trade in the town of Kenmare.

"Education really starts when you leave school, and some of the smartest men the world has ever known had little education. There was a man I knew who had only a poor schooling, but had used his time well all his life. One day another man came to him who had travelled the world, and they got talking. But the man who had travelled had travelled with his eyes and his ears closed, and was no wiser when he came home than when he left. He was pitying the man who had stayed at home, but he was too good for him.

"'Travel', said he. 'I've travelled more of the world with the light of a penny candle than you have done in all your years of travelling.'

"I was bound to a tailor. I had to pay a fee of nine pounds

and have two indentures and serve for five years. It was hard work, and I had to work hard. You may be damnful sure that I did. Till ten or eleven or maybe sometimes twelve at night on two meals a day, and that a thin diet.

"It is done now, but I would not care to do it again. The worst time was at Christmas. The whole world would be wanting clothes then. You'd think that no one wore clothes at all except on Christmas Day, there was such a rush for them.

"The only holidays were Sundays and holy days. At Christmas you would be left off from Christmas Eve till the morning after St Stephen's Day. The devil a fear but you had few holidays and hard times in those days.

"Up in the morning at six, and work on until ten at least, except for the two bits of meals. And the meals, to make the most of them, did not cost above half a crown in the week. Food was very cheap then. Two loaves of bread for fourpence and a stone of sugar for one and fourpence. Not a drink, and no talk about it. You would not handle a penny from one end of the year to the other. You got nothing beyond your training and your meals and your bed.

"There was an apprentice, bound as I was bound, who had to get up and dig the potatoes and wash them and cook them for the breakfast. When they were ready he would call the master and the mistress. They would come down then and pick the best of the potatoes.

"The apprentice would get what was left in the skihogue by the door, and would have to sit on the floor and eat them. That was his breakfast, and that was his table. What he left the pig got.

"Well, one morning when he was eating his breakfast this way, the sow put her head inside the door and took a bite of the potatoes out of the basket. The apprentice jumped up and took a stick and beat the sow out.

" 'Blast you! Get out!' said he. 'If it is the same diet we share, it shan't be at the same table.'

"Such were the times. That was the way the world was going and those were the times I lived through.

"After five years you were at liberty, and you didn't give a damn. You drew your indentures and went away as journeyman.

"I stopped in Kenmare for a time with a man by the name of O'Connor, and I went from him to Killarney. I was there about four months or five. You would not stop long in one place at all. You would get very small pay in these small towns. 'Tis all that you would get would be six to eight shillings a week and be fed.

The master tailor himself would get no more than ten shillings for the making of a suit.

"From Killarney I moved to Cork. When you went into a city like Cork you worked by a different system. You would be either a coat maker or a pants maker. It was all what was called 'piecework', and you would make good money at it.

"You would make thirty to forty shillings a week and sometimes maybe sixty. You would get board and lodging and washing done for ten shillings a week, and good too. Yerra, manalive, the money then was worth three times as much as it is worth nowadays. Two ounces of tobacco only cost sixpence, and you would get a half-gallon of porter for eightpence.

"Cork was a great place at the time. There was a constant work. There were no factories, and no women working. Everything in those days was tailored, and there was a heap of wealthy people in Cork. Gentlemen in those days would buy as many as nine suits at a time.

"I was in Cork for some time, but after a while I thought that I might as well be seeing something of the world, so I struck away for Waterford, and that was the beginning of my travels."

The chorus takes the stage again.

"Travels! Listen to him and his 'travels'. The divil a bit does he travel away from his ould box by the fire. He'll be stuck to it one of these days. 'Travels'!"

Chapter Nine

We were sitting on the side of the road, watching the world go by. Cork Echo came up the hill with a heavily-laden cart drawn by a jennet. After a few words he passed on.

"Do you know," started the Tailor, settling himself comfortably on the wall, "that the jennet is the most willing animal in the world? Manalive, a jennet never knows when he is done. Years ago, I saw a jennet drawing a load up Patrick's Hill in Cork, and that's like the side of a mountain. The load was too much for it, and for all its trying the jennet could go no farther.

"But do you know what happened? With the height of willingness and the power of pulling, its eyes came out of its head before it, for they were the only part of it free and not tackled to the cart. That was willingness for you!

"The man who owned that jennet was carrying from Cork to Kenmare. It was in the days before there were any motorcars and before their like had been thought about at all.

"He was coming one day with the divil of a load of wheat, maybe it could be about a ton weight, and he saw that his horse was failing. He wondered if he had overfed her or what could ail her. He wanted to get into the town of Macroom that night at least.

"Well, he had a bottle of poteen with him, and he put it back into the horse, and she was as lively as could be for another piece of the road. But just when he was to the east of Macroom, didn't the horse lie down on the road, under the load, and the divil a stir from her.

"They thought that she was dead. There wasn't a move out of her, no matter what they did. One of the men with him said that they had as well make the best of it, and if they skinned her they would be able to sell the skin in Macroom.

"So they set to, and they skinned her, and when they had that done she moved. She wasn't dead at all, but only dead drunk with the poteen she had taken, and the cold had put a stir into her when the skin was off.

"They were in the devil of a fix, for the skin was after stiffening. One of them had an idee. There were sheep grazing in a field near by, and he hopped over the wall, and killed four of the sheep and skinned them, and they sewed the warm skins on to the horse, and she got up after her debauch, and pulled away as good as ever.

"Ever after that he used to shear her twice a year – and you should have seen the grand fleece she had on her. She lived for fourteen years after that with two shearings a year.

"Ah! The divil blast the lie is it?" he adds, noticing the look of incredulity. "Wasn't I often speaking to the son of the man who owned her?"

A proof which would have scarcely satisfied Euclid.

"The nature of animals is one of the most curious things in the world. The way birds fly from here to Africy: how a cat finds its way across country: how the salmon comes out of the sea and finds the fresh water in the spawning season: and how the eels all find their way to the bottom of the sea off the coast of America, all these things are mysteries to me.

"Then there is the intelligence of rats and foxes. A man might be trying all his days to beat them, but they will beat him in the end. The only way to beat them is to kill them. All these things have some learning and some curious ways of knowing that we cannot understand. All my life I have wondered about these things, but I know no more now.

"There's another curious thing happening. There's a change in the animals, if you only look about you and take notice. Years ago you could leave young ducks and chickens out at night, and they would come by no harm. The rats would not touch them. Scarcely anything would touch them. But nowadays, damn it, they are scarcely safe if you take them into bed with you at night.

"Last year I saw something of this that started me thinking. I saw a 'johnny the bog' (crane) doing something that I had never seen nor never heard tell of before. The 'johnny the bog' is the most harmless bird with wings you'd think. They would fish away for themselves and do no harm to anything else.

"Well, by the mockstick of war! I was standing here of a day and I heard a screeching down by the bottom of the land, and I went to it and I found that it was a 'johnny the bog' pecking at a young duckling, and it killed it. That was a thing the like of which had never been heard of before, and I would not believe it if it was told to me, but that I saw it with my own eyes.

"It was last year, too, that I saw a rat and a weasel fight here in the middle of the road, opposite me out. There was nothing strange in that, for I have often seen them fight before. They fought and they screeched until the weasel had bits made of the rat. There is nothing of the size could stand up to the weasel. They are the Dane's cats and limbs of the devil himself.

"The curious thing was that when he had his piece of business done he turned round to go to his burrow, and I was standing in the way. He looked at me in a terrible fierce sort of a way and stood there staring at me. Afraid? The divil a bit was he afraid. Do you know that I thought then, and I think still, that he had a mind to attack me, and I do not know why he did not. I threw the stick at him, but he made no more of that than a bull would of a daisy. He stood still and stared still at me. I don't know how long it went on. Then he turned away and went slowly another way as though he had changed his mind.

"There is a change somehow. The animals are getting more daring and more intelligent. They are thinking more and they are learning the way we think too. They are not stupid. It is we who are stupid to think that they are stupid.

"I've wondered sometimes if there is just so much intelligence in the world, and if we don't use it the animals get the use of it. And people do use intelligence less than they used to do in the old days. It may be so, for this world is curious, and there is more in it than meets the eye.

"Did you know that it was because of the instinct of an animal that the indigo dye first came to Ireland?

"I'll tell you the history of it, and divil a lie is there in it, though most people won't give in to it.

"Years ago there was a boat came into Bantry harbour, and the captain of it came into the town. He was on his way from India. He had a few drinks and fell into conversation with some of the people in the town, and got intimate with them.

"He was a decent, conversible type of man, and, as the evening was coming, they asked him to play a game of cards, and he said that he would as he was staying the night anyway. They were playing for some time and the light was failing as the night came. One of them lit a piece of a candle and put it on the table. But with the banging and the thumping of the cards in the excitement of the play the candle kept falling down.

"Then one of them said that he would go and look for a sconce, but the captain of the boat said 'No', for he had a better sconce than any one they could find in Bantry town.

"He had a bag with him, and he pulled the bag from under the table and took out a cat. He put the cat sitting at one end of the table and put the candle between his paws. It was one of the neatest bits of business you ever set eyes on. All the town came in to look at it, for they had never seen the likes before.

"The captain explained to them that he had trained a cat in this business, for when they were playing cards in the Indian

63

Ocean there were terrible rough seas, and no candle would stand up for them.

"All the town marvelled except one man, who said that it was well enough, and he had admiration enough for the captain and for his cat, but that nature was a greater thing than training. The two started an argument, and they almost came to blows. Then they decided to bet a wager on who was right. The captain bet a cargo of indigo blue that learning was greater than nature, and the man from Bantry bet a farm of land that nature was stronger than learning.

"They carried on with the game, and when it was over, the captain put his cat into the bag and went away with himself to bed. He stayed the following day, and that night they all played cards again, and the cat was at the end of the table with the candle between his paws.

"The man who had the wager bet with the captain was playing too, and half-ways through the game he took a mouse out of his pocket and put it on the table. As soon as the cat saw it it dropped the candle and chased the mouse, and the man from Bantry won his wager and proved that nature is stronger than learning. The captain paid him the cargo of indigo dye, and that was how the indigo first came to this country.

"All my life I have heard that a white hazel stick drives away snakes. They are afraid of it. It has some power over them, and they won't come near to it, and you won't see them. But I have never been able to test it, for St Patrick drove all the snakes out of this country.

"Last spring there was a man came to see me who had a job, under the British Government, in Nigeria, which is near to the 'white man's grave' on the coast of Africy. He was telling me about the place and the work he does there. He told me that he liked it well enough, but that the snakes there are middling plentiful, and that they are terribly fierce, and a bite from them would kill a person.

"I told him that what he needed was a white hazel stick, such as I use myself, and before he went back I cut such a stick for him and trimmed it and sent it to him. I had a letter from him a few days ago. He tells me that when he walks round the camp they have there, he always carries the stick I gave him, and he has not seen a snake since he returned.

"People will not give in to these things and they go against common-sense, for these things do be. The tokens are there, and the tokens are there for anyone with two eyes in his head to see, and the tokens are terrible.

"I'll tell you another thing about the white hazel. Do you see

64

this stick in my hand? Do you see that it has flat sides? Now go to the door and you will find another stick of white hazel and you will see that that is round entirely. One is from a female tree and the other from a male tree. All trees are male or female, but it is best seen in the white hazel. It stands to sense. Where you have breeding you must have the two sexes. Doesn't it say in the Book that 'God made all things, male and female'?

"There are people who walk through the world who see nothing and hear nothing and learn nothing and know nothing. I don't know why they are alive at all. There are animals learn quicker and have more sense than a deal of human beings.

"I saw a curious thing in this line myself a few years ago. Did you ever know that a sow is a very intelligent animal?

"I was on the road to this side of Turendubh. There is a pool there at the side of the road, and a 'johnny the bog' had caught an eel in the pool and was swallowing him. The 'johnny the bog' is a strange kind of a bird. He has only a straight gut.

"Well, he was swallowing the eel and he wasn't making much of a hand at the business, for the eel ran straight through him, and the 'johnny the bog' kept swallowing him and losing him again.

"Johnny Jerry had a sow at that time and she was always on the side of the road. She came along and she stood for a while and watched the 'johnny the bog' go through the performance several times. Then she made a grab for the eel herself and swallowed him and clapped her backside up against the wall!

"Now wasn't she a cute and a quick scholar? Yerra, don't be talking. A man can see a new wonder every minute of the day, if only he has the intelligence to know a wonder when he sees one."

Chapter Ten

The Tailor's imagination is highly inflammable. A word will set it blazing. His memory is a storehouse to which the most trivial phrase is a key.

"Kind and civil." "Kind and civil," said he, "like the beggarman long ago, who came to the door of the old woman and said, 'Good lady, would you be so civil and so kind as to give me a coal to conflagrate my pipe, and we will smoke it in conjunction.'

"They were smart and witty in those days.' They had the ready answers and the ingenuity. Nowadays you seldom ever meet a man who has any talk in him. You may as well be talking to a bush at the side of the road as to most people.

"Living is like a man fishing with a seine. He throws his net into the sea, and then hauls it home with his catch. But the catch isn't much use to him unless he gets rid of it and sells it. If he keeps it, he gets no profit. It goes bad on him. That is what happens to a deal of people. Whatever they catch in their net goes bad on them.

"It was not so in the old days. A man exchanged his catch with his neighbour, and there was plenty, and plenty of variety for all. There was more poetry in the old days, and there were more poets and better poets. I remember long before I ever saw the first pair of bellows for blowing up the fire, hearing it described this way:

> My back it is deal,
> My belly's the same,
> And my sides are well bound with good leather.
> My nose it is brass,
> There's a hole in my ass,
> And I'm very much used in cold weather.

"There is no one nowadays could give you such a witty riddle about a bellows. Those were the airy times and the good times, in spite of the hard living. But there was plenty of fun as well.

"I was telling you the other day about the match-making and the weddings they used to have. There was another end to the business as well. All things have an end as well as a beginning. A man's beginning is in how his mother met the man, and his end is in the wake.

"There were great wakes in the old days, but a lot of the customs of wakes are dying out now. The people have other sorts of amusements and do not pay as much heed to the old ways as they did. But I don't know that they do any better for themselves. I've been to some damn fine wakes in my time, faith I have.

"A wake would last for two days. There would be pipes, grand, cool-smoking clay pipes, such as are not made now. There would be a pipe for each man, and he would help himself to tobacco from a plateful which would be there. There would be snuff for those who did not take the tobacco, and bread and butter and tea, a half-tierce of porter and whiskey.

"It was whiskey, too, in those days. There would be none of the stuff they sell in the public-houses today. It would be a disgrace. There would be real whiskey, some of the first run of it. A man knew that he had had a drink when he had that taken.

"When the man was dead, the first thing they would do would be to send for the 'keeners'. They were a class of people who would come to the wake, and make a recitation about the man, and kick up the hell of a noise. It was the most pitiful noise in the world. They would tell what manner of person the dead man was; how he lived and how he died, and you would hear them bawl and cry until you thought that the last day had come. If they were not fairly paid, they would dispraise the dead man. They would cut him down to dirt.

"The neighbours would come in and say prayers, and talk, and have a smoke and a drink. There used to be a lot of drink taken sometimes at a wake, for it was a lonely time. Sometimes the people got very airy. I remember to my dying day a wake I went to years ago and what happened there.

"There was a young child in the house, and out in the middle of the night it started to bawl, and nothing would stop it. The women of the house were upstairs and they would do nothing for it.

"There was a man at the wake by the name of Sullivan, Michael Sullivan. He was a great copper-coloured tanyard of a fellow, over six feet tall and one of the airiest men that ever walked. Well, by the hokey, the baby was getting no better and it was spoiling the fun, so Mick got up from where he was sitting, and he took the baby in his arms and walked up and down the kitchen, from the hearth to the dresser, and he started to sing. This is the song he sang, for it was the only one he knew:

67

Woman of the house, I'll kiss your daughter,
Every time she goes for the water.
Woman of the house, I'll kiss your daughter,
Every time she goes for the water!

"Up and down he went, singing his song, and the neighbours killing themselves with the height of laughter, until the baby was quiet again. I'll remember that as long as I live.

"There was an Englishman about here years ago who was clean mad to see a wake. He was writing a book, and he wanted to put a wake into it. But there was no one dying at the time, and it looked as though he would be disappointed and never be able to finish his book.

"He was a decent, friendly type of a man, and you would like to please him and help him all that you could. We were talking about him one night, and he was a pity by us, and we arranged to have a wake for him. We planned it all, sitting here by this fire, unknown to him.

"The corpse was to be a man by the name of Kruger, which was a kind of pet name we had for him. He had a farm there across on the other side of the valley. He lived alone, and he was a damned airy type of a fellow. The poor fellow is dead now – may the Lord have mercy on him.

"The following day we told the Englishman that Kruger was after dying during the night, and was to be waked that night, but was so badly off that it would only be a very poor class of a wake. There would not be money enough for even a half-tierce of porter to wake the poor fellow decently.

"Well, the Englishman said that it was a pity, and that he would like to help him to be waked properly and decently, and he gave money for the half-tierce and for whiskey besides. We got the whiskey and the half-tierce and pipes and tobacco as well. We got everything ready and had everyone ready and told them the plan.

"We asked the Englishman if he would come with us that night to the wake, and he said that he would. So we faced out for Kruger's. When we got there, Kruger was stretched out on the table and there was a sheet over him and his face was chalked. There was only a poor light in the room, and that away from him. All those who were in the plan were there already. There were keeners, kicking up the devil's own row, and everything that was necessary to give the dead man a good send-off.

"We tapped the half-tierce and sat down to make a night of it. We told stories about Kruger – what a good class of a man he was. Now and again someone would tell a story to try and make the corpse laugh, but Kruger was a stout man and never batted an eyelid.

"We'd made an arrangement that out of every round from the half-tierce we put aside a basinful for Kruger for when the wake was over, and you could see him watching that he got his fair dues. When the half-tierce was empty, and the company was getting mellowed, we started on the whiskey.

"The Englishman wasn't used to this, for it was the right whiskey, and soon he was getting pretty 'young' (merry) and enjoying himself with the best of us, and thinking a wake to be a damned fine piece of business altogether, and not knowing whether he was in heaven or hell. We had songs and recitations, and all was going as well as bedamned until one fellow started to take a sup out of Kruger's share of the drink.

"The corpse spotted him, but did not say anything the first time. The second time he moved on the table, but the Englishman did not see him, and someone told him, in Irish, to be quiet and not be spoiling the fun.

"But it was no fun for Kruger after all. He was the corpse, and it was his wake, and he was watching everyone else enjoying themselves, and he had not even tasted a sup of the drink. Being a corpse was thirsty work, you may be damful sure.

"When the fellow went at it for the third time, Kruger could stand it no more. He jumped up off the table and threw the sheet off him and upset the candles so that they went out, and stood, bare naked, and bawled:

"'Thon amon dieul! Johnny Paddy, I always thought that you were a thief, but I had to come back from the dead to find you out.'

"The Englishman let out the devil of a screech, and skedooed out of the house as fast as his legs could carry him. We never heard tell if he finished his book, but we laughed ourselves sick over the wake. I tell you that that was one of the airiest wakes that was ever known.

"There was something like that happened at another wake years ago. They were waking a man who was found dead, sitting in a chair, and he had got stiff and his body was bent as he was sitting. He looked queer on the table with his knees sticking up. But if you pressed his knees down the rest of his body came up from the table.

"Well, the divil a bit, but someone devised a plan for settling the business and to keep him straight. They tied a rope round his knees and under the table, and another round his chest, and he looked as decent a corpse as ever lay on a table then.

"The wake went on, and a piece of the night was spent, and

people were getting lively, when some boy cut the rope round the corpse's chest, and he popped up off the table as though he had been shot. The company thought that he had come to life again, and there was the devil's own hullabullo.

"Yerra, manalive. Those were the airy times. It was worth being alive in those days. A man would enjoy all the day through, and when he died he would be the better for living. It was work hard and live hard, and the great enjoyment.

"But I must tell you more about the business of waking. There used to be a lot of queer superstitions attached to wakes and funerals. After the wake the coffin would be taken outside to put the lid on it. Then the first four men to lift it should be of the same name as the dead man. There were no hearses in those days. Wherever the man was to be buried he would be shouldered the whole way.

"As soon as the corpse was lifted from the table, one party would be on the watch to turn it over, and the other party would be watching not to leave them do it. The belief was that the party who would turn it down would keep the death away from their side of the family and put it on the others.

"This often developed into a fight, and a heavy fight. I have seen this question settled myself many and many a time. But it is a custom that is not much seen nowadays. All that is done is that the table is stirred out of position."

Ansty comes in. She hears the last phrase and echoes it into a question without any interest at all.

"Whyfor was the table stirred out of position?" Then her eye catches sight of the fire, which is almost out.

"Put a sod of turf on the fire or what ails you! Sitting there all day with the 'witchawatcha' and the talk. Nothing but the talk and the shtories! Put a sod of turf on the fire as I tell you!"

The Tailor stirs himself leisurely, and rakes over the embers and starts to sing:

I am a gay young bachelor in search of a wife,
In hopes that she will be the joy and comfort of my life.
If anybody asks me I tell them it is true
That I'm going to get married –
                              When I've nothing else to do!

When summer's tasks were over and when winter's rains did
            spout,
In search of a sweetheart I instantly set out.
Down to a cottage that I had long in view,
For I got a zeal for courting –
                              I had nothing else to do!

70

I warmly saluted her, and down by her I sat,
For a time we were discoursing and giving each other chat.
She liked my conversation till something else got in her view,
There she got a zeal for courting too –
                    She had nothing else to do!

You're a handsome young fellow, and it's my heart that you
        have won,
And there's only one remedy for all that we have done.
If you will prove as true to me as I will prove to you,
We will go and get married –
                    When we've nothing else to do!

I gave my consent along with her to roam,
Just as soon as Father Donovan happened to be at home.
We put in our tenders to make one of us two,
And he buckled us both together –
                    There was naught else he could do!

And now we are married and we live in sweet content,
Like many of our neighbours we have no reason to lament.
To our friends and relations we both have bid adieu,
And I can kiss my pretty girl –
                    When I've nothing else to do!

Chapter Eleven

You never know who you may meet in the Tailor's. Today you may go in and find "Dan Bedam" scratching his head over some yarn of the Tailor's. Tomorrow you may find a touring American whom the Tailor invited in for "a heat of the tea". Another day it may be the sergeant of the Civic Guard or a "travelling man" who will stay the night.

In the summer you will find the "Saint" doing feats of dexterity with his sixteen stone weight on the chair of honour, and rousing Ansty to the utmost limits of her abuse. For one week in September you are sure to meet Morgan, a farmer, who walks over the mountains when most of the year is done, to spend a week with the Tailor. "The best holiday any man could ever wish for," as he describes it.

At some time or other you will come across them all. The Sheep, Cork Echo, and all the rest of them. There is one that you will never meet in the flesh, but whom you will meet often in the Tailor's affectionate memory—Jerry Cokely. He will speak of him oftentimes as though he was vividly present, and there is seldom a day passes that some recollection of him does not float through the Tailor's mind.

His whole countenance lights up in joy at the thought of him. "Jerry, my boy, the greatest saint in all Ireland. The Lord have mercy on him. He was a great soul. If only he was here now.

"He was a fierce, tall man. He was five feet eleven at least, and big accordingly, and a powerful worker. Many and many is the day he gave here with me working, and many and many the night he sat here talking. Many is the pot of potatoes we dug and boiled and ate together, and many the half-gallon of porter we drank together.

"We talked together and we laughed together and we quarrelled together, too, at times, for there were times when he would quarrel, but it would soon be over and forgotten.

"He lived by himself in a little old thatched hut he built for himself down by the cross, and it is what he had for a window in it was the end of a bottle. We had many a bit of sport at Jerry and his window.

"Thamwirrashimfaina! I remember the time that he had a

72

fierce row with a groom, that used to be at the cross when they had the coaching stables there. That was in the days of the horse coaches, and they would change horses there to come up the hill. In some way Jerry had upset the groom, who was only a small class of a man and no match at all for Jerry.

"The groom was as angry as a cornered rat and did not know what to do. In his temper he shook his fist at Jerry. 'Thon amon dieul! But before the day is much older I'll . . . I'll . . . I'll break every window in your house!'

"Jerry used to wear no coat, but a 'bawneen' and white flannin drawers. He had a bloody fine 'brusher' (beard), the finest you ever did see, and he was always stroking it. He used to make a living of a kind by selling bog oak sticks to the visitors to the island, and by showing them round and telling them lies. He used to work with the farmers about, too, when he felt like it.

"One of the lies he would tell was if anyone asked him about miracles. He would point out the ruins of an old house across the lake and tell them that there was a man born there, years ago, who had seven noses. Each September he came to the 'pattern', and each year one of the noses fell off him. He gave up after the sixth year and had nothing more to do with religion. You can have too much even of religion if it is going to cost you a nose.

"When he was young he had slept out under a May moon, which is one of the most dangerous things any man can do. Any moon is bad, but the May moon is the worst of them all. It always affects a man's brain. Isn't it the divil of a thing that if you had the height of that table of clothes under you, when you slept out in the early part of the year, the sign of the grass would be all over your body?

"It affected my saint in his speech. He would turn words backwards. It was not a joke. He could not help it, as though his brain was changed round in some curious way. He would say 'telhot' instead of 'hotel' and such-like.

"He was never very much good at the English, but he had the grand Irish. It was the best Irish any man ever spoke; and he was a great talker with it. He was never at school in his life and had no book education, but he could manage to read in a sort of way. He had a lot of the old traditions, and the old poetry, and the old sayings, and the old wisdom. He knew the gospels by rote in Irish better than any priest, and he was a very religious man. He also had all the prophecies in his head, and was able to use them too.

"I'll remember the queer way he had of talking till I die. He would say things such as 'it would not rain again for ten futures' if he thought that the weather would hold fine for a long spell. One day the two of us were in the town of Macroom of a fair day. He saw the notice over the police barracks, and he read it out in his awkward sort of a way. 'Royal . . . Irish . . . Constant bullery!' 'Saint' said he to me, 'We must go in and see that. That must be a fine performance!'

"Thamwirrashimfaina! Jerry, but you were the great soul, and there's none of your kind in the world today, and the world is a poorer place since you left it.

"He'd be alive yet if he gave himself proper justice; but he was careless about himself. He would not have proper food, and he would not take care of any sort of an ailment he had, and there were times when he would drive the devil of a spree."

" 'Pon my soul! That's true for him," corroborates Ansty. "Didn't I come across him one day when I was going up to the well for water, and it was out in November and, oh! glory be, don't be talking, but the rain there was! It was a miracle. And there was my Jerry lying in the ditch at the side of the road, and the water pouring over him and he singing away, and I had to pull him out, and he was a big, heavy man."

"Why didn't you get the Tailor to help you?"

"Get the Tailor to help me? Get the Tailor to help me, indeed! Yerra, the Lord save you, wasn't that divil lying in the ditch at the other side of the road!"

The Tailor does not mind. He was in good company.

"Jerry, my saint, had a cat, which he called the 'Moonlighter'. He was very fond of it, and he would talk to it, and the cat would understand it. Certainly that cat had sense. Tell me the cat that has not. Jerry used to tell a story himself about how sensible the 'Moonlighter' was. I don't know if it was true, but I will tell it to you as it was told to me by Jerry himself.

"Jerry was a great poacher, and one time, when the salmon were running up the river in the spawning season, Jerry and the 'Moonlighter' went out for a night's sport. Jerry was a great artist at getting a salmon out of a river. There was none better.

"Jerry took one bank of the river and the 'Moonlighter' took the other. Jerry did fairly well at the game himself, and after a while he counted up and found that he had put out eleven.

"He called over to the 'Moonlighter', 'How are things going with you, saint? I have eleven myself.'

"The cat turned round and counted his own share of the night's work, and he found that he had eleven, too. What did he do but in with him to the river and out again with another salmon in his arms, making twelve and one the better of Jerry. I tell you, that cat was no mean scholar.

"When the 'Moonlighter' died, Jerry was heartbroken. He

thought that he was his only friend in the world. He waked him for two nights and two days. It was a right proper wake, too. There was tobacco and pipes and whiskey, and the 'Moon-lighter' was laid out on Jerry's own bed. Then he buried him in a box, and put up a headstone to him.

"There was great nature in the man, and you could not help but sympathize with him. It may be that the people we think to be mad are the really sane ones, and it is we ourselves who are mad.

"There was great nature in him, and great sense in him, too, when you came to understand his queer way of putting it out. He had a deal of sense to him. At one time he had a bit of a donkey car, and he would be drawing out turf from the bogs with it and doing bits of jobs.

"At that time the police were very busy catching people travelling without lights. They had nothing much to do other-wise, and I suppose they had to earn their wages. Well, Jerry was late leaving the village one night, and he thought that maybe the police would be out on the road against him, and would find him without a light.

"What do you think my saint did? He untackled the donkey and tied him behind the car, and himself went between the shafts and drew it. That would be nothing at all to him, for he was a strong, powerful man. He pulled away home, and the donkey followed on behind.

"The police did come out to him before he had gone much of the road. One of them stepped out from the side of the road in the dark and asked him, 'Where is your light?' All Jerry said was, 'Go behind and ask the driver,' and pulled away.

"The first time that Jerry saw a motor-car was at the bottom of Carrigadreen. He looked at it in astonishment, and the man driving it asked him if he had ever seen the like before.

"'No,' said Jerry. 'I have not, but I knew that you were coming. It is in the prophecy that a coach without a horse would travel the road.'

"'This is faster than any horse,' said the man.

"'It is not,' said Jerry, 'nor is it as fast as a man.'

"'The divil fire you!' said the man then, 'how can you say a thing like that? Will you race me up to the lake for a gallon of porter and we will make a trial of it?'

"'I will,' said Jerry, 'if you will go the nearest way.'

"'All right,' said the man then, and got back into his car.

"Jerry hopped over the fence and started to strike out the near way over the bog.

"'Yerra, blast you!' said the man, 'where the hell do you think you are going?'

75

" 'Blast you!' called back Jerry. 'I am going the near way. Follow you after me.'

" 'How do you think that I can go that way?'

" 'I don't know, but that was the wager we laid down.'

"The man saw that Jerry was too good for him. 'You've won the bet,' said he, 'but no man ever travelled that way except on foot before.'

" 'Oh, yes, there was a man travelled this way before, and it was not on foot.'

" 'Who was he?'

" 'It was Noah,' replied Jerry, 'when he sailed over the earth in his ark.'

" 'Did you know, Noah?' asked the man of the car then, thinking that he would have some fun with Jerry.

" 'I did not, though he was my brother,' Jerry answered him.

" 'Your brother? How could you be Noah's brother? Are you so old?'

" 'I am not so old,' replied Jerry, 'but aren't we all, the whole human race, brothers and sisters to our Father who is in Heaven?'

" 'I thought it was a stump of a fool that I had met,' said the man then, 'but I find that I have a wiser man than myself. Jump in, and we will go up to the hotel and settle the wager.'

"When Jerry died, I was damned lonesome after him and I am yet. I miss the times he would come in here and talk or work. We used to pull together greatly. But we all have to go in the end, and all that we can do is to make the best of living while we have it, the way the saint did. Enjoy life and do no man any harm. The world is only a blue-bag. Knock a squeeze out of it when you can.

"In the latter end he was taken to the county hospital, and he died there. There was a sort of obstinacy in him and he would not see sense in some directions, and he would not take care of himself or do himself right justice.

"When he died I went for him. I hired a sidecar, and we got a coffin in Clonakilty and brought him back and buried him in Inchigeela. I'll remember the day ever. It was in November and terribly wet the day we brought all that was left of my saint back.

"I'll remember how lonesome it was sitting there with my hand on Jerry's coffin, and thinking that he would not be there in the spring for the planting of the potatoes, and he would not be there to cut the turf for me, and he would not be there to eat the goose with me and drink the punch at Christmas.

"I watched him being covered up by the wet, cold earth, and I came away home by myself. For a long time afterwards I used to listen, expecting to hear him coming up the road, singing, for he was always singing. Sometimes at night I used to expect to hear him open the door and hear his voice in greeting. But he never came – the greatest saint in all Ireland and the best man that ever a man could meet."

The Tailor is on as good terms with the local civic guards as he is with everyone else. You will often find one of them "having a heat of the tea", or drying his clothes on a wet day before the Tailor's fire and rousing Ansty.

The Tailor's attitude towards the law is definite enough. He does not mind how harsh the laws are made. They do not concern him unless he has a notion of breaking them. There are, however, certain loopholes in his armour. He finds the taste of a salmon which has been poached as good, if not even better, than one which has been caught according to the law. An account in the paper of a poteen raid and the spilling of the "wash" rouses his indignation, and he calls to heaven to witness this mortal sin.

In this he stands upon tolerably firm ground. These are only man-made laws. There are laws beyond the temporary laws of man. Why should the drinking of whiskey on which a tax has been paid be right, and the drinking of whiskey on which no tax has been paid be wrong? Why should the fish of the streams be any particular man's property, and why should there be a legal and an illegal means of killing them? There can be little difference between the two ways from the fish's point of view, or between the taste to the man who eats them.

So if you are a particular friend you may be offered some day "a sup from the bottle". It is an involved procedure. The question is mooted and discussed with becks and nods between Ansty and the Tailor. Ansty plays the role of Hebe on this occasion. She goes out first to inspect the lay of the land, and returns to report.

Then she journeys out again and wanders round from place to place with the art of a corncrake in a tour of deception. For the bottle is hidden somewhere within the acre or on the bounds of the acre. It is in some secret place in a hole in the wall, or the fence, or a crevice in the rocks, or between the drills of the potatoes. The mountains which surround are full of eyes, and one can never be circumspect enough.

After the campaign of deception, she brings the bottle in, and its contents are hurriedly dispensed. It is poured into cups or tumblers, whatever may be handy. All the time that the bottle is in the house there is anxiety in Ansty's mind and eyes. You are urged to drink it up quickly. You may not desecrate it with water, but Ansty will permit the addition of a little milk.

You cough and splutter and choke as the fiery liquid burns your mouth and throat, and trickles down to your stomach like a red-hot lava flow. The Tailor tosses his back with the abandon of long usage.

He smacks his lips. His eyes light up.

"Wisha! But that's grand stuff. As soft as mothers' milk. Not like the fiery stuff they sell in the public-houses for whiskey. That is stuff that would do any man good. There's a great curing in it, and no man who drank that would ever be sick."

"Hould your blather, you ould shtal, and drink it up. You don't know who might come into the yard," commands Hebe.

"As soft as mothers' milk!" Maybe you think, as it sears and scorches you, the milk of the dragon or the salamander must be something like this. But that is not the end of the ritual. Ansty snatches up the bottle, and wraps it up in the folds of her apron, and returns it to its hiding-place with the same secrecy with which she approached it. Only Ansty knows where it is. One can keep a secret, but you can't be so sure of two.

She returns for the conclusion of the ritual. The tumblers are scrupulously rinsed and smelt lest any trace remain. Then Ansty lights a piece of rag in the fire and wafts the smouldering offering about the room. When at last the room is well filled with the smoke of burning rag, then, and only then, does the anxiety fade from her face.

What with the rag smoke and the volcano within you, and the Tailor's description and the anxiety of Ansty and the hurry, you wonder where you are and what may happen next. The Tailor has not half the worry. He treats the matter altogether too lightly. He even jokes about it all. Perhaps that is the reason why he does not know where the bottle is kept.

"Yerra, no. The old R.I.C. were a decent enough body of men in their way. They had a job to do, and a difficult job. You'll find good and bad amongst every class of men, and you can't condemn the lot for one. The old sergeant from the village used often to resort here, as the present sergeant does, and spend a piece of the day talking.

"He was a tidy, decent slip of a man, and I liked him well, and got on with him well. I remember one day he came in, and we got chatting about the news of the day. Well, after a while he said, 'Tim, duty is duty, you know . . . and Tim . . . orders are orders.' He was a shy kind of man, and he had a kind of impediment in his breathing, a sort of asthma, and he used to have to pause for breath after every few words.

" 'We got orders this morning, Tim ... orders from Dublin Castle, Tim ... I'm sorry to say, Tim ... orders to search for poteen, Tim.'

" 'Yerra!' said I, 'that's bad news. It couldn't be worse.'

" 'It is, Tim,' said he, 'but ... a man must do his duty, Tim.'

" 'True for you, Sergeant,' I said.

" 'Would there be a drop about the place, Tim?'

" 'There might and there might not, Sergeant,' said I.

" 'Tim ... I'm thinking that in case there is ... we'd better drink the evidence first and ... make the search afterwards.'

"Now wasn't he the decent man and acted like a true gentleman?"

"Was I ever telling you about the jury case we had up at the hotel? It wasn't really a trial, but a coroner's inquest, but they had a system very much like a trial in a court-house. There was a jury, and they had to listen to the evidence, and find out what had happened to the man and give their opinion.

"It all happened over a man who was found dead on the island. He had fallen over a bank, and a slab had fallen on top of him and broke his neck.

"Well, the following morning the coroner and the sergeant came along, collecting a jury. There were twelve of us. There was the Sheep and Cork Echo and Dan Bedam and the Rocky Mountaineer and several others. Some of them are dead now – may the Lord have mercy on them.

"There was a priest once preached a sermon on the twelve apostles, and it was failing him to describe what type of men they were at all. He wanted to tell the people that they were just ordinary folk: that there was nothing grand or smart about them. So after he had thought for a while he said, 'They were twelve working men. Farmers and fishermen and such class of people. They were twelve ignorant men – as ignorant as any twelve men you would find in this parish, and, God knows, that wouldn't be difficult.'

"Well, the twelve apostles were like the jury we had that day – as ignorant as any twelve men you would find in this parish. The divil a bit but we all assembled, and we struck away up to the hotel. They hadn't an idee what was going to happen to them. Some of them thought that they were going to be tried for killing the man. Others thought that they were going to his wake. And more of them thought that they were going to 'shoulder' him to his grave. You see it was the first time that there had been a jury case in the district for many a long year, and it was all a mystery to them, for none of them, except myself, had ever travelled.

79

"Good enough! We got to the hotel, and the body was lying in a room, and we all had a look at it. The poor fellow was dead enough. There was no doubt about that – God rest his soul. The coroner asked if we recognized the man, and we did, for he was well known to most of us.

"After we had all had our fill of the sight, we had a couple more drinks, and then we went into the room where the case was to be tried. There were chairs for each of us, and the sergeant and the coroner were there.

"The sergeant told the others that they would have to take the oath and swear on the book. Then Cork Echo spoke up. He hadn't said a word till this. He said that he would not swear, because swearing was a sin, and he started quoting bits out of the catechism. He wasn't going to swear with his eyes open. It would be altogether different if he did it unknownst to himself, but he had not enough drink taken yet.

"The sergeant started quoting bits from a book he had in his pocket, and then the coroner joined in, but they were only making a poor hand of the business. I explained it to him and all about the business, and that battle was done with.

"To save time we held the book in threes, and took the oath together. When it came to Dan Bedam he said that he wanted to swear alone, and he would not put his hand on the book with anyone else. So he swore alone. He held the book as though it was going to bite him, and when he had his swearing done he looked behind him as though he expected the devil was there waiting to take him.

"The sergeant and the coroner got their note-books ready, and we were all set for the business. Just as we were going to start, the Sheep got up and started to go out. The coroner wanted to know where the hell he thought he was going, and the Sheep explained that he was 'going behind', for he had drink taken and his bladder was weak.

"So we waited for the Sheep to return, and when he'd returned and sat down and lighted his pipe we started again.

"The sergeant read his statement, and we listened. Then the man who had found the body told how he had come to find it, and the coroner asked if we accepted that.

"The year before the man who had found the body had sold the Rocky Mountaineer a mare, and the mare was faulty. The Rocky Mountaineer did not find this out until after the deal was made, and he could do nothing but wait till he got the chance of his man again, and this was his chance.

"I declare to God, didn't he say that the man was a liar, and that there was no one there at the time but him, and he might have pushed the man over the wall. Well, they had a few words,

80

and the sergeant called the meeting to order, and the coroner was not able to make out what had happened till the sergeant explained the affair to him, and then the coroner understood and the business proceeded.

"The coroner explained what had happened, and what sort of a verdict we could bring in – either death by misadventure or *felo de se,* or murder by person unknown, and he explained his own opinion.

"The Rocky Mountaineer jumped up, and said it was plain murder, and he did not care a damn what anyone else said, for he had had dealings with the man who found the body, and he had swindled him over the sale of a horse, and if he would do that, murder was nothing to him. So we had that all over again.

"It was a very warm day and the room was small, and what with the smoke and the arguments we decided that a drink or two would not do anyone any harm. So we retired for a drink or two, and when we came back we took up the business where we had left off. The coroner counted and found one missing. 'Sky high', who was one of the jury, had not come back. The sergeant went off to find him, and found him on his way home and brought him back. He said that it wasn't in his line at all. That he did not understand it, and he had a cow at home that was due to calve, and he would be better there. But the coroner made him stay.

"The coroner talked to them about *felo de se,* and he explained all about it to us. When he had finished, Dan Bedam got up and said that he could not understand it at all. How could the fellow fall into the sea, he asked, when the sea was fifteen miles away as the crow flies?

" 'Bedam, I couldn't agree to that at all. Bedam, it could be "fell into the lake", but, bedam, it could never be, "fell into the sea".'

"The coroner explained again, but Dan Bedam could not understand him still.

" 'Bedam, if the fellow fell into the sea he would be wet, wouldn't he? Bedam, but his clothes were quite dry. Bedam, it couldn't be that at all, but some other thing.'

"The coroner explained suicide, too, but Dan Bedam had not heard of that either. He wanted to know if it was Irish. In the middle of this argument there was a knock at the door, and in walked 'Ball o' Wax's' wife with his dinner.

"She's the divil of a great pounder of a woman, who would make a grand door for a car-house. 'Ball o' Wax' is only a small class of a man, but he had a fierce appetite, and his wife was afraid that he would die if he did not have his dinner. He was a great friend of Dan's, and the two of them started on the dinner and forgot all about the inquest. Not that it mattered much, for the two of them were ever better at eating than they were at thinking, and the wife had brought up a grand 'potash' of pig's head and cabbage and potatoes.

"At last the business was coming to a head, and the coroner asked us to consider our verdict. Then the fun started. One said one thing and one another. The effects of the drink had worn off the Rocky Mountaineer, and he was all for murder again. The Sheep said that he did not understand it at all, and he would not care to give his opinion. That was with the height of meanness. He would not even give his opinion unless he was paid for it.

"Cork Echo thought that the business was all wrong, and that no good would ever come of it, and the less we had to do with it the better. He had not got over the swearing part of it yet. I tried to knock sense into their heads, but it was failing me.

"Now that Dàn Bedam had a bellyful of food he had an idee.

" 'Bedam!' said he, 'doesn't the man say that it was death by misadventure? Bedam! isn't he from the Government? Bedam! it would not be right to agree with him so. We must say something else, bedam!'

"There were others of them with queer notions, and there were some of them so scared stiff that they were just sitting like dummies and saying nothing at all. Twelve good men and true! Am Bostha! you'd search the earth before you would find an equal pack of mugwumps of bladdergashes!

"I went to the coroner, who was a decent, sensible type of a man, and explained the position to him. We sent the rest of them into the bar for a drink, and I and the coroner settled the business, and we brought in a verdict of death by misadventure, and I added a vote of sympathy with the poor fellow's relations in their trouble, and we left the jury to drink itself stupid. But they could never do that if they were drinking to this day, for they were stupid before they started.

"Twelve men, as ignorant as any twelve men you would find in this parish, and God knows that would be easy enough – with their weak bladders, and their sins, and their cows calving, and their pig's head and cabbage, and their 'fell in the sea'!"

Chapter Twelve

It was a day before the threatening storm had broken over Europe. The Tailor was busy with a pot on the fire, puffing and blowing as he stirred it.

"What have you there, Tailor?"

"Wait," he commanded, as though the question was the interruption of a mystery, and continued for a while with his brew. At last it was finished to his satisfaction, and he got up.

"I am going to settle this business in Europe," he announced invitingly.

"However are you going to manage that?"

"By the power of hocus-pocus and Lily Page's Liquid Glue. That's the Lily Page's Liquid Glue," he added, pointing to the pot. "It is the most powerful glue that was ever in the world, and I am going to put it on the soles of Hitler's boots and Mossoline's boots, and when they put them to the ground, they will never be able to move again. But that isn't all. I am going to give them a basin of stirabout with the glue mixed through it, and after the first mouthful they will never be able to open their mouths again. The divil mend them but I'll settle them. They have gone obstropelous entirely."

That was his joke; but when the war came, it did touch him even in the safety of the deep glen in the Irish hills. He thought of his friends all over the world, and the hardships they would suffer. He wanted to send butter to his friends in England and Scotland, and when Denmark was invaded the war came much nearer home, for "Kissten" was in Denmark.

"Kissten" became his friend years ago while she was touring Ireland. After the first night in his cottage, when she had sat and listened and said nothing, he was not impressed favourably by her.

"Do you know," he said, "there was a poet called Shakespeare who wrote a play about a Dane, and he called him 'the melancholy Dane'. And do you know that I think he was right?"

But then he came to know "Kissten" and to like her, and he recanted. He discovered a lot in common with her. "After all, weren't the Danes in Ireland for hundreds of years? Didn't they leave the grouse, which was their hen, behind them, and the

83

weasel, which was their cat, and the hedgehog, which was their pig? Didn't we teach them all about pig farming and dairy farming, so that they have come to be the best farmers in the world today?"

There was one thing he could not get from "Kissten". It was the formula for "the Danes' drink", made from the heather. "Kissten" had not even heard about it, but the Tailor suspected that she knew but would not tell. For the last two men who had the secret in Ireland went to their death rather than disclose it.

"The soldiers came at them and captured them, and tried to get the information out of them, but neither of them would tell the secret. They tortured them, but no good. Then one of the soldiers thought of a plan. He said they would kill the son before the father's eyes, for they were father and son, thinking that they would make the father tell.

"Well, they started, and they did kill the son, and the father didn't bat an eyelid. 'The devil fire you now,' said the father, 'you can do what you like. I only wanted him out of the way, for only he and I had the secret' – for they were working a still together – 'now you will never know, for I am the only one left who knows.'

"They tried all sorts of ways. They tortured him, and they watched him, and they were as soft as cream by him, but devil a word did they ever get out of him, and he died, and the secret died with him, and he was the last of the Danes in Ireland.

"That must have been one of the most powerful drinks that have ever been in the world, and I'd like to try a sup of that before I die."

"Kissten" tried to make recompense for her ignorance or her secrecy by sending the Tailor seeds for cabbage trees, which he set, but which the rabbits ate. But the memory of "Kissten" remained, and still he wonders how she is, and if she has enough to eat, and will he ever see her again.

It was a glorious Sunday morning in September when Chamberlain declared war on Germany. The Tailor was perched on one of the ivy-covered rocks of Garrynapeaka, sunning himself and "minding the dairy herd", when the news was brought to him. He was silent for a while.

"Haven't I often said that I am a wise man? There are my potatoes and cabbage. There is the cow and the hay to feed her. There is a pig hanging from the ceiling in the kitchen. A millionaire in the city of London may not know where his breakfast is to come from in a year's time – and whatever a man may think, he must eat."

The situation has grown a bit too vast and complicated for him now, though each evening he and Cork Echo discuss it, and each day Ansty asks, "How's the war?" as though it was a case of measles.

Cork Echo is one of the regular nightly visitors. That is not his real name at all, but the Tailor's nickname for him because of his curiously prophetic knowledge.

"Thamwirrashimfaina!" exclaims the Tailor, with a trace of envy, "that man must be in league with the devil. How else would he come to know the things he does know? Or else he is a freemason," he adds, as a further possibility.

Very much of the Tailor's as well as the local interest in the war revolves around "the prophecies". Up in the mountains lives an old man who is known as "Dan the Prophet". He does not himself prophesy, but is reputed to have the "books" in his possession, but no one has ever laid eyes upon them.

They are the prophecies of St Malachi, St Odranus, St Columcille and MacAuliffe. Their origin is very doubtful, but, though doubtful, they are not less accurate than the belauded "experts", who kept Europe informed before the event. They are, too, a little more succinct and poetic than the dicta of the readers of the stars in the daily papers.

They are usually quoted as "what the old people said" or "what the old man said long ago", or "it is in the book that". They are current in Irish, but the Tailor interprets them and translates them into English.

"Ireland will be seven years a widow, without either king or head."

The Tailor interprets that as the period 1914–22, from the shelving of the Home Rule Bill until the founding of the Irish Free State.

"A time will come when you will not care to live in Cork, Bandon, or Kinsale."

That period is the period of the Black and Tans in Ireland, and refers to the severity of their rule in these three towns.

"A Spaniard will free Ireland." That is obviously de Valera.

A later period in the history of Ireland is contained in: "There will come a time when you will carry your stuff to the market and the bag will be worth more than the contents."

The ingenious interpretation of this, according to the Tailor, who, if not the prophet or the guardian of the prophecies, is the interpreter of them, is that this was a reference to the time of the Economic War with England, when a calf was only valuable for its skin and the flesh was valueless.

There is a general prognostication of the times in: "The trout will grow small in the streams. The young men will get grey before their time. The women will lose their shame."

The prophecies and the sayings of "the old man" are not restricted to Ireland. They apply generally to Europe. It is chiefly through them that interest is maintained in the war, where there are so few evident signs of it.

Before the war the Tailor often said that war would come from the East. It would come in the year when the Palm and the Shamrock were worn together on the same day. Palm Sunday and St Patrick's Day fell on the same day in 1940.

"It is East the long dance will start, and England will pay the piper."

"The French will make a false peace that will take the head off England."

"The old man would be turned three times in his bed" (to see if he was fit to fight).

"A time will come when there will be snowy nights and bloody blankets."

"That London will be burnt to the ground."

"That a woman would stand on London Bridge with her young daughter, and her daughter would point and say: 'Mother, look at the man.' " (A man would be so rare.)

"That such a law would come in this country that the Irishman would cry on the Englishman's grave." (The law would be so harsh compared with the English law.)

The capitulation of France gave these prophecies great authority, and put them beyond the range of question. They are the end of all arguments and the foundation of all news.

"I tell you that there is more in them than you think," asserts the Tailor in support. "The old people had knowledge and wisdom, and they did know the way the world was going. The tokens are there as plain as the nose before your face, if you only have the sense to read. The tokens are there, and the tokens are terrible.

"They had a damn fine way of telling them, too. They were poetry and they were witty at the same time, and they needed understanding. You had to have knowledge yourself to make them plain. But the old people were ever like this. Wasn't I telling you their way of reckoning land – the collop? Wasn't that a better way than the present way?

"They had a way, too, for reckoning time which was better than 'years and centuries'. It was reckoned on the things a man could see about him, so that, wherever he was, he had an almanac.

"It was written down in Irish, but I will put the English on it. It starts with the rail of a fence, and goes on to the age of the world:

"A hound outlives three rails.

"A horse outlives three hounds.

"A jock outlives three horses.

"A deer outlives three jocks.

"An eagle outlives three deer.

"A yew-tree outlives three eagles.

"An old ridge in the ground outlives three yew-trees.

"Three times the time that the sign of a ridge will be seen in the ground will be as long as from the beginning to the end of the world.

"It's a pity, and a mighty pity, that all the old learning is being lost, and that nothing better or the equal to it is taking its place."

But the war is a long way still from Garrynapeaka. No sign of it, beyond an increase in the price of tobacco, and the loss of some of his visitors, has touched the Tailor yet. Aeroplanes are still a rare sight and a wonder. Tanks are as vague as dragons. Air-raid shelters are fantastic.

The Tailor takes little interest in home politics. He votes when there is an election, but the glory has faded from politics nowadays. There is no national cause, no Parnell, no William O'Brien, no Moonlighters, no evictions, no grabbers to bring politics close and vividly home.

At the last election he recorded his vote for the labour man. The clerk of the poll, the schoolmaster, was explaining the procedure to him, but the Tailor cut him short.

"I voted before you were born, and for better men than there are in the world today."

He treated the referendum on the Constitution with indifference and a certain wisdom.

"If you think that I, or any man, can answer 'yes' or 'no' to all the articles of the Constitution you are wrong. I have not read them, and I know few who have, but I do know that there are parts of it I agree with, and parts of it that I disagree with. Damn it, man, a man doesn't have to eat all that is on his plate – meat, and fat and bones as well."

During the campaign for the election, the Tailor went into a public-house, where two young men were discussing the rights and the wrongs of voting over a pint.

One was arguing that he saw no sense in voting a man into a good job when he had never seen the man, and that what did we want a government for, anyway? and further still – until he had worked himself up into a temper.

The Tailor listened and finished his drink. As he passed out, he touched the local anarchist on the shoulder.

"You were wondering what the hell we need a government for at all. Do you know that I am inclined to agree with you? The only use of governments, so far as I can see, is to govern people who can't govern themselves – such as yourself."

An hour or two later he returned to the same bar and found the same two still at the same argument. The Tailor ordered his drink and drank it at his ease. When he had finished he turned to the two, who recognized him.

"I have not come back here to talk politics with you," he said. "This place was built for better use than that. I have come to teach you philosophy by means of poetry."

Then he sang a song, and the bitterness of political discussion was banished because the Tailor is a wise man and practises what he preaches. "The world is only a blue-bag. Knock a squeeze out of it when you can."

War and politics can affect him little. He is both wise and rich. Wise because he knows that life is too short for a long face—and it may all be a joke. Rich because he knows that there are few things worth the effort of gaining. He has all that the world has to offer, in essence. "A man can only sleep on one bed at a time. There is nothing makes food so good as hunger. Treat the world fine and aisy and the world will treat you fine and aisy."

"People think nothing of going to Cork nowadays. . . . They think less of going round the world than the old people used to think of going to Cork. There is a great change come over the world, and I don't know that it is for the better.

"Do you know that I often heard my father say that, and I suppose that you will say that in sixty years' time, and I suppose that Noah said it to his sons. I suppose that we all get kind of dotty when we grow old.

"Yet there is truth in it all the same. People travel much oftener and much farther and know less. They go journeys too quickly, and see and hear nothing. They are mad to be where they are not. They neither learn anything at home nor on their journeys.

"The old people stayed at home and journeyed round their own doorsteps, until they came to know their own place thoroughly. If a man knows his own doorstep well, he knows a deal about the world already. Then when they made journeys they were slow journeys, and they had time to see and hear and think and learn, so that they came to know both ways. That's the difference.

"When I went to Cork it was a very different place to what it is now. The streets were all coarse stone, and on a wet day there would be floods and the gutter would go up to your knees.

"I never cared much about living in Cork or in any city, but I made the best of it. I went to the opera and whatever else was going. They had pictures of a kind then, and they were very poor. Not much more than a glare of light on a sheet. On Sundays you would go to Youghal or Cove with comrades. If you were courting a girl you would take her away on the route with you.

"I was lodging with a fellow who was supposed to be studying to be a doctor, but the divil a bit of study did he do beyond the study of the bottom of a glass. I found great occupation at night studying his books, and I came to learn a deal that way and better my education.

"From Cork I went to Dublin. That was a much bigger place. I saw the King of England while I was in Dublin. That was a fine sight. It was as good as any circus coming down the street.

"From Dublin I went to Belfast, and from there to Scotland—"

"What did you think of Belfast?"

"Yerra, nothing more than Dublin. It was a city, just in the same way. From there I went to Scotland—"

"But haven't you some impressions of Belfast? What did you think of the people?"

"They were all right in their way. From there I went to Scotland—"

"Haven't you anything else to say about Belfast?"

"The divil a bit else," said the Tailor, with an unusual curtness and haste. "From there I went to Scotland. I went to Glasgow, and I was in Ayr and Maybole and Kirkoswald for four years.

"I liked Scotland, both the place and the people. They were a very obliging and decent people in every bloody way. There were differences in customs and food, though the food was simple enough. There'd be a pot of potatoes thrown out on the table, and you would have sour milk with them. You would get a bellyful of them and off to bed with you, and after that a man would have no more worry in the world till he was hungry again.

"They had grand beer in Scotland, but not much stout. They had plenty of whiskey, but it was chiefly manufactured whiskey. They did not know the real whiskey. The women were very fine too. Jolly and merry and full of fun.

"I settled there for a while at my trade. Then I did housekeeping for some comrades of mine who were working on the building of a railway. I was in Glasgow and I went to Loch Lomond. Yerra, you should see the mountains they have in Scotland! They must be the highest mountains in the world.

"After four years I took a notion to be moving again, and I found my way back to Cork, and I worked there for a while. Then I found my way out here, and I decided that it was coming time to settle down. So I got married, and I have stopped here ever since.

"I had a notion once to go to America. There were a lot of friends and relations of mine going there and were there at that time. But the notion wasn't strong. I don't know what would have happened to me if I had gone. I might have been made the President of America, but it was not to be. A man meets what is coming to him and he cannot avoid it. But I would not have minded being the President of America. I would have made some good new laws for them.

"There was a man from that side of the mountain opposite who went to America some years ago. There was a mission on at the time in the village, and as the people were coming home from it they saw him walking west with his boots under his arm.

"He wasn't seen for some time after that, and people were wondering what had happened to him. They were thinking, maybe, that he had fallen into a boghole and got drowned. But the divil a fear did he get drowned. Some weeks later someone got a letter from a brother they had in America, to say that he had met Micky MacCarthy, that was the man's name, walking up the High Street of New York, and he still with his boots under his arm. He said that he was after walking from West Cork and was feeling a bit tired, and was looking for a place where he could get a night's lodging."

"He walked from here to New York? How on earth could he do that? The Atlantic Ocean is in between."

"Yerra, manalive, he went by way of the Eution Auction Islands" (the Aleutian Islands?), explained the Tailor.

"The Eution Auction Islands! Where on earth are they? I have never heard of those."

"I always thought that you were a little bit backward. You only looked at the face of the map. They are printed on the back side of it. You want to examine things a little bit closer in future. You wouldn't look at only one side of a pig if you were buying her, would you?

"Wisha! there's no wonder in that at all. Do you know! when I was in Scotland I met a man who had walked all the way from England! From England to Scotland, mind you!

"Travelling. Travelling! There is no man can realize the difference there is in travelling nowadays to the old days. No one had ever thought of a motor in those days, and aeroplanes were sheer madness. But they were all foretold in 'the books'. 'The old man' knew all about them, but we paid no heed to them then. Just as we pay no heed to him now, though all he says is coming true.

"My father was only in Cork once in his lifetime, and when he had that done he thought he had a great thing done, and that he was one of the wonders of the world. But people nowadays go to Cork and forget they have ever been there. There are aeroplanes that can travel at five hundred miles an hour, and Cork is not fifty miles away. So they would be able to go to Cork in five minutes, in the time it would take you to walk as far as Johnny Con's cross. I am wondering what will happen if they go any faster than this. There will come a time when they will get there before they start, and they will be in a nice fix then. They won't know which way they are facing. They will be having their dinner before their breakfast, and they will be getting up before they go to bed.

"When my father went to Cork it would take him the better part of a week, going and coming. There's a difference for you! Perhaps that is the reason why the people nowadays get old and grey before their time.

"There was a fellow long ago lived west, in Castletown. He wanted to make a journey to Bantry by the mail-car which used to run in those days.

"The mail-car pulled up at the post-office to take on the mails, and, begod, Jerry – Jerry McNally was his name – went into the post-office, too. He asked for a penny stamp, and when he got it he stuck it on his forehead and climbed on to the mail-car again and came on away with it into Bantry.

"When he came off the car in Bantry the driver said to him, 'You pay me five shillings for carrying you from Castletown down here.'

"'What the hell do you mean,' said McNally, 'by charging me five shillings?'

"'Five shillings is the charge,' said the mail-carman, 'for the journey from Castletown to Bantry.'

"'The divil blast you, man,' said Jerry to him then, 'don't you see that I am travelling by post? I'm stamped.'"

A couple of years ago the Tailor visited Cork again with the Saint, but the change was too vast for him. So many of the old landmarks had gone, and the face of the place had changed so much since he was there before that he was lost.

He searched for a public-house called the "Hollybush". If only he had been able to find that he would have been able to take a bearing, and to know that he was in Cork again.

"They had the best porter in Cork City. If only we could find the 'Hollybush' it is there that we would get the pint, and we would have 'a dog's leg' and anchor there!"

But the "Hollybush" was not to be found. No one seemed ever to have heard about it. Though we had many pints they were all only invidious reminders of the excellence of the pints at the "Hollybush", and nowhere could we find "a dog's leg". We might as well have gone to Tokio. It would have been no more foreign than Cork of the present day compared with the days when the Tailor knew it.

The Tailor has his own valuation of places and of people. One day someone gushed to him about Killarney and their impressions of the place. He listened for a while. It seemed a waste of enthusiasm to him, for he had lived amidst such scenery nearly all the days of his life. When the torrent of enthusiasm was working out, he stepped in.

"Tell me, did you come across any fleas there?" he asked. "Killarney was always famous for a breed of fleas they had there. Though I was often there myself, and lived there for a while, I never saw them, and I wondered if it was just a piece of advertisement. A friend of mine, a pig dealer, told me he saw one of them, but he was near a Killarney man himself. His mother was from the place.

"He told me that one of them bit him in the bed by night. He threw off the bed-clothes, and the flea jumped out, and was trying to get out of the window. The pig dealer made a swipe at him with his boot, and the flea barked at him. Did you come across the breed while you were there?"

"That for 'oo! Always the shtories out of the shmoke! Better for 'oo to let the cow out and talk afterwards. . . . The rabbits are getting into the garden. . . . They'll be in the yard soon . . . and 'oo sit there . . . talking and laughing and shmoking your ould pipe." So interrupts Ansty after a long silence.

But the Tailor is not disturbed. "Yerra, what harm," he replies. "They will be crossing the hens next, and we'll be able to start a circus with the produce. And I'll be able to put you in, too. You'll be able to do tricks with a bicycle.

"Did you ever hear of the man who was his own grand-father?" asks the Tailor, suddenly remembering it and as quickly forgetting Ansty. "He'd have been a great man to have in a circus. He'd have been a Klondyke. Well, it did happen, and I will tell you how it happened.

"I was telling you some time about the match-making business. Well, this happened over a match. It was years ago it happened in Kerry, bedamned.

"There was a widow woman had a daughter. She wasn't too old herself, for they used to marry at an early age in those days. The match-maker came to her and told her that he thought that the daughter would make a good match for a son of a friend of his. The widow woman was agreeable to consider it, and they appointed a place and a time for the meeting.

"The father of the boy was a widower, too, and he was middling young himself. The widow woman and the widower got on well together, and the match was going ahead. They met again and it was looking as though all was settled. And all was settled, but not the way people thought.

"For the father of the boy was thinking that it would do him no harm to get married again. There was still a frolic in him. The mother of the girl was thinking it would be lonesome when the daughter had gone, and she could still raise a caper. The business of the match set them both thinking. Well, by the mockstick of war, it all ended in a double wedding. The father and the son and the widow and the daughter all got married on the one day.

"You might say that there was nothing strange in that, but wait till I tell you. The father of the boy married the widow woman's daughter, and the boy married the widow woman herself.

"So far so good. They got married, and there was a great wedding. The daughter stayed at home, and the son went to her, and the widow went to the father's farm. After a while they had small lads, both of them. I told you that the widow woman had a caper left in her still. It was then they got into the divil's own fix.

"For you see the widow woman's child by the son was the grandson of the daughter's husband. And the daughter's son was stepbrother to the widow's husband, and the son's wife was the grandmother of the son because she was his mother's mother, and he was his wife's husband and her grandchild, and so he was his own grandfather!"

"Hould your whist! you divil, with your lies and your planning and your mother's mother. Why don't you say 'Lord have mercy on them'?" intervened Ansty, in the cause of propriety and respect.

"The Tailor paid no attention at all to her.

"I tell you but they would have made a grand start for a circus. 'One-night Duffy' would have given his ears to have them. I expect that they are dead now – the Lord have mercy on them. I never heard what happened to them in the end – but it's true. The divil blast the lie is it.

"I have just remembered something about Killarney. It is a sort of riddle I heard many years ago. Do you know what we look for, and when we find it we throw it away, and when we don't find it, we keep it?"

We made all sorts of guesses, and all were wrong, to the Tailor's great glee.

"Thon amon dieul! What poor scholars you are! Fleas, of course!"

"It's the nice talk you have," chips in Ansty again. "Pity you can't find something else to talk about but – fleas and your mother's mother."

The company broke up.

"What did happen in Belfast, Tailor?"

"Well, I'll tell you now, but you have to be careful to whom you tell certain things. There are people who see ill in anything at all, and I didn't like to tell you while that old 'hairpin' (one of his guests) was listening.

"I was in Belfast with some more of the boys from Kerry, and the people there knew it by our speech. There are a class of people there called the Orangemen, and they are very bitter against Catholics. There is a river runs through Belfast called the Lagan, and there are bridges over it like over the Lee in Cork. Well, by the hokey, one night didn't some of these Orangemen come up to us and told us to say 'to hell with the Pope!' "

"Yes, and what did you do?"

"We refused and pitched them to hell, of course. Weren't we Kerrymen? But there were too many of them for us, and at last they got us by the legs and hung us head down over the bridge, and the Lagan flowing beneath us. They told us then to say 'to hell with the Pope!' "

"Yes, and what did you do then?"

"I did a bit of quick thinking. I thought – well, they can always get another pope, but there is only one me!

"I'd like to see the old 'hairpin' hanging head down into the Lagan and see if she would be making a holy martyr of herself."

Chapter Thirteen

The day was ended. All the labours of the day were done. The shutters were drawn across and the door was closed against the night. The lamp on the wall was lit. The sign of all these things was that Ansty was at last still, and was sitting by the fire gazing into the heart of it.

"People do often say that a man who is smart is as wise as King Solomon, and I have always heard tell that King Solomon was the wisest man that ever lived. But I have always had my doubts about that too," mused the Tailor.

"You see he had ten thousand wives, and I can't put the two things together rightly in my mind, so that they make sense."

"Ten thousand wives! Glory be!" echoes Ansty, automatically.

Then she repeats it. "Ten thousand wives!" A note of interest has come into her voice, and she wakes up from her fire-gazing. Slowly she reckons up on her finger-tips, ignoring the thousands, for thousands are in the domain of heaven and hell and London and America. They are merely words. They do not exist. She counts back the ten again and springs into activity.

"Ten thousand wives! Hould, you ould divil! It's your beads you ought to be telling instead of your jokes."

"I've reckoned it up, and no matter how frolicsome a man might be it would take him nearly on thirty years of nights, without having any holiday at all, to get his conjugal rights from the lot of them."

"Thirty years of nights? Without a holiday? Glory be!" Ansty ponders, bewildered by the powers of reckoning. "Thirty years of nights, and he a king? ... King!" she spits with contempt. "King, am bostha! That wasn't a king. He must have been an ould tomcat. ... Thirty years of nights! The Lord save us."

"Of course, being a king he could get what help he liked, but what the hell was the use of that? That only makes matters worse and makes him out to be a bigger class of a fool still. What sense is there in a man getting married if he is going to let someone else have all the fun? So I have never been able to make out rightly if he was the wisest man or the biggest damn fool the world has ever known."

"Thirty years of nights!" still echoes and swirls around in Ansty's mind. She chuckles to herself and repeats the phrase again and again. "Thirty years of nights! Ring a dora!"

"Then he must have been pretty busy besides, for kings were no fun in those days. They had a lot to do."

"No fun in those days? Gon rahid! Have you taken leave of your senses entirely? Thirty years of nights. Ten thousand wives. And he says they had no fun in those days! That for the senseless talk by him who thinks he's the whole push. No fun in those days, indeed!" Ansty is almost paralysed with contempt, but the Tailor pays no attention at all to her. The conversation is on a plane far above her level.

"There was a friend of mine by the name of Paddy Sullivan who went to Algery, which is a part of Africa, called the 'white man's grave'. He was in the British Army. When he came back we were talking about this very subject one day, and he was telling me that there was a sort of a king out there. They called him the Rajah Ben Salam, and he had a hundred wives.

"Paddy was telling me that he saw them with his own eyes, but he could not get nearer to them than that. Rajah Ben Salam had a lot of men looking after them – a queer kind of men, like wethers. I don't know, and Paddy did not know either, if they were born like that or if they had been 'burzeroed' the way you would do sheep—"

"And himself the ould ram by them, I suppose?" adds Ansty.

"That must have been the devil's own job – like trying to hang your hat upon a rainbow. But these heathens are terribly cruel people. Only they could think of a thing like that. I have often thought that perhaps they were men who had committed some crime, and this was the way of punishing them – but it was a terrible way. The man who would do a thing like that could have no heart at all.

"This man, Rajah Ben Salam, was black, and most of the wives were black, and Paddy was telling me that the black women are much easier to handle than white ones. That must be. For one white woman is enough for any man. Then the heat must make a difference, too, for it is terrible hot in Algery. But still there is a lot of difference between King Solomo and his ten thousand wives, and Rajah Ben Salam and his hundred wives. A power of difference."

"A hundred wives! A hundred wives!" The figures have come down from the domain of astronomy within the range of Ansty's comprehension. "Hould, you divil! Leave me alone with him and his 'hundred wives'." The position has become completely absurd now. "A hundred wives! Listen to him and his lies!"

"Marriage is a strange thing when you come to look at it rightly. First of all a man is clean mad to get married, and then when he is married he wonders what the hell happened to him."

"How well you got married yourself," asserts Ansty.

At last the Tailor pays attention to her.

"Thon amon dieul! was there ever a day since that I didn't regret it?" he asks, as though the question was barely worth asking. "Anyway," he adds after a pause, "I was only 'alludin' '.

"The system in this country for marriages was ever 'the match'. It still is, though there are some of them nowadays who get married for love. From Christmas out to Shrove there would be 'matches' and talk of 'matches'.

"The system was like this. A man who had a son who was ready for marriage would think of a girl who would make a good wife for him. She would have to be a good milker and have a 'fortune' and come of respectable people. He would come to know of such a girl and send some other man to start the business. It might be a friend of his, or it might be someone who made a business of match-making.

"He would go and speak to the girl's father, and say that he was sent by such a one and what his business was. I remember years ago a man who went match-making, and he made a speech and he learnt it by rote. I'll remember it as long as I live, for it was a pretty, witty class of a speech and I helped him to make it.

"This was what he said to the father of the girl: 'I was sent here this morning by a good, decent, respectable boy who has the grass of three cows and three cows on it. He has a heifer and a bullock with that. He has a large flock of sheep and a good plot of turbary. He is of good, decent, respectable family: well educated, well reared in the bad times: a steady worker, put to all farm work and free from luxury, sedition and all other vicious habits.'

"Well, if the father of the girl was agreeable to the match, he would make an appointment to meet the father of the boy at a certain public-house at a certain time. They would meet and have a few drinks and the father would tell the fortune he would be expecting with the girl. They would try to cut each other down on this, until they came to an agreement.

"The next part of the business was what was called 'walking the land'. The father of the girl would come to the boy's house, and they would have porter and whiskey ready for him, and they would have a drink together. Then they would have a look at the land to see if it was good land, and at the house to see if it was in good repair. They would have a look at the cattle and everything in the place, and the father of the girl would dispraise everything. Then they might come to terms again on the fortune and have another drink, and perhaps spend the rest of the evening card-playing and singing and drinking.

"The fortunes that were going in the old days with any girl who was any good would be twenty cows and a bull. That would be the highest going. She would be the top of the country. There would be no such thing as money then, but always the cattle, which was a kind of money.

"There would be a sort of an agreement written by someone who was a bit of a scholar. There would be any amount of clauses written into it. One would want this and the other would want something else. The old couple would keep a room in the house during their lifetime. They would keep a cow for milk and should get so many potatoes in the year – dug, manured and set. And so many crates of turf in case of a disagreement, for you could never tell until after how a marriage would turn out.

"Nowadays the solicitors draw up the agreement, and they draw it up pretty tight and strong, and they do well out of the business. Nowadays it is mostly money that they have for 'fortunes'.

"When that battle was over the couple would get married, and the priest would get a share of the fortune for marrying them. Maybe one cow or two cows, or the price of them more likely. That wasn't the end of the business.

"Maybe the man who got married would have a sister. More than likely in the old days, for they had families then, I can tell you. Ten and twelve and sometimes more. I remember there was a man in the place where I came from who had only a very poor way of living, and he had seventeen in family.

"There was a wealthy farmer near by who bought a bull. It was the finest bull that was ever seen in Ireland, and people were coming from all over the country, when they heard about it, to see the famous bull. There were so many of them coming that the farmer was charging them a shilling, for he had something else to do but be showing everyone his fine bull. But that did not stop them. They were mad to see it, and the farmer employed a man to take the shillings and show the bull.

"Well, by the hokey, didn't this man with the seventeen in family come to hear about it and he wanted to see the bull. But a shilling was a lot of money to him. He went to the farmer and he explained who he was, and what his condition was, and he asked the farmer if he would let him see the bull for sixpence.

"'Not at all. Not at all,' said the farmer. 'Put your money in your pocket and wait there. I am going to bring the bull out to see you!'

"Where was I? Oh, yes. I was telling you about the man after he got married. Well, if he had a sister she was to get married. Well, whatever the brother got as fortune with his wife, his sister would get as fortune, and she would clear out of the place and leave it to him. When she got married the priest would get some more of the fortune, and the fortune or the twenty cows and a bull would go round and round as fortune like money, till the priest got the lot of it. It was like a shilling, and every time it changed hands the priest got a penny out of it.

"If the man who got married and had no family coming to him, and there was another boy in the house, the farm would be handed over to him and he would get married to see if he was any better at the business. There was sort of a disgrace in the name of a place changing. There must always be the same name on the land, and that could not be unless there was a family coming to the man who had the land.

"There was a custom, and there still is, called 'The Skellig List'. Someone who was a poet in the neighbourhood would write a long rigmarole about all the young people who were of age for getting married and were not getting married. They would tell all the news about them so that everyone would know. They were witty pieces of business.

"Another custom they had at weddings, but which is dying out in some parts of the country, was 'The Straw Boys'.

"Whenever there was a wedding, about twenty of the young men of the place would get together and make suits of straw for themselves. They were damned clever dresses, for they would cover them so that you could not tell who was wearing them. They would go to the wedding. They would sing and take out some of the girls and dance a set and do no harm at all. They would ask nothing, but take what they were given. The first thing a person would ask about a wedding would be, 'Had they the "straw boys"?'

"Yerra, there used to be some fierce weddings in the old days. There'd be sixty pounds of fresh beef. Four or maybe six stuffed geese. A tierce and a half of porter and five or six gallons of whiskey. Wisha! when I got married myself I had a tierce of porter, and up to sixty people in the house singing and dancing."

"And himself 'paishted' so that he did not know whether it was a wake or a wedding he was at!" comes the comment from Ansty, who has been silent for a long time.

"Paishted! What 'paishted'! The devil a bit of difference is there between a wedding and a wake if you look at it properly.

"They had some queer customs in the old days," mused the

Tailor. "They were some queer people and they had some queer ways. Though they had more sense in a deal of ways than the people that is in the world today, they were more like children. They knew some things and they did not know others.

"I remember a couple who got married and were married for seven years and were not 'producing'. John and Joan were their names."

"Married seven years? . . . and not 'producing'? . . . The Lord save us! . . . As flat as a board after seven years? . . . Ring a dora!"

"As flat as a board," repeats the Tailor with contempt mixed with his mimicry. "As flat as a board!" he repeats with emphasis of Ansty's stupidity. "As flat as the palm of my hand, if you please!"

Ansty is momentarily stunned with the vehemence of the Tailor's assertion.

"The queer notion they had," he continues, "was that John should slap Joan in the belly with a pair of breeches, in the name of the Father, the Son and the Holy Ghost, whenever they got the idea."

"Wisha!" snorts Ansty, filled with disgust, "that was the queer carry-on. With a pair of breeches? . . . Glory be!"

"Then someone told them the trade, and I tell you that they fell to at the business and they made small lads as fast as you would count them almost."

"With a pair of breeches! . . . With a pair of breeches!"

"I tell you that it is a queer business altogether. There are those who want small lads can't have them, and those who do not want them have them. Women are like cattle. There are some of them will breed for you if you only look at them, and some of them go to the 'pusher' time and time again and won't have any calf."

"If you only look at them?" repeats Ansty incredulously. "Yerra. There's not much fun in that."

"I was only 'alludin' '. Have sense, woman. Have sense."

Ansty's mind is set at ease again, and she returns to her study of the heart of the fire, and the Tailor wanders round from one thing to another until there is a stir of departure.

"Ten thousand wives! . . . If you only look at them. . . . Glory be! . . . It's a fine, bright night. Good night now – and mind the steps as you go out. . . . Ten thousand wives. . . . The Lord save us."

Chapter Fourteen

Amongst the Tailor's many friends is Seamus Murphy, the Irish sculptor. When he proposed making a bust of the Tailor, the Tailor readily agreed, and was ready for the job on the spot.

"Damn it, man, it was ever said that two heads are better than one, and the one I have now I have had for seventy-five years and it is getting the worse for wear. Of course I'll have a new one."

All the apparatus and materials were assembled, and the Tailor inspected them with the interest of a fellow craftsman. Ansty ignored the business in the beginning. Her only interest in it was her resentment of the invasion of the Room – "with all the ould clay and mortar to make a new divil" – and making fresh disorder of her disorder.

The Room at last justified the Tailor's name for it, and did become for a while "The Studio". For an hour or so each day he posed and talked and commented. The measurements interested him and he linked this part of the business with his own craft.

"Many's the time that I have measured a man's body for a new suit of clothes, but I never thought that the day would come when I would be measured myself for a new head."

"I think that we will have a rest for a while," suggested Seamus during one session.

"The divil a rest do I need. Do you know that I feel it less than I did the time the whole of my body was making before I was born. There is a considerable improvement in this method. A man can smoke and take his ease and chat away for himself."

The news soon spread that the Tailor's "image" was being made. Even the Sheep, on his weekly visit, mentioned it.

"I did hear tell, Tailor, that you are in the way of having your 'image' made. I don't know. But I did hear tell."

"Faith, I am," agreed the Tailor, "and a good strong one too. It is going to be made in bronze – the hardest metal that ever was. It was the metal that the Tuath de Danaans brought to Ireland with them, and it will last for hundreds of years."

"Indeed!" exclaimed the Sheep, settling down a little farther on his stick. "Tell me, Tailor," he asked, with a show of interest, "how will that be done?"

"Yerra, manalive. It's easy enough. You stick your head into a pot of stirabout, and when it is cold you pull out your head and melt the metal and pour it into the hole your head made. Then you eat up the stirabout and you find your new head inside the pot."

"Indeed!" grunted the Sheep. "Indeed, that's wonderful enough." He settled a little more securely on his stick to absorb and digest this new information. After a while he came out of his shell again. "They tell me that it is unlucky for a man to have his image made, Tailor. Would this be like a photograph now, could you tell me?" The Sheep has always refused to stand for his photo.

"Thon amon dieul! Unlucky! It isn't half so unlucky as going to bed. Many a man had twins as the result of going to bed, and, anyway, most people die in bed. If they had real sense they would keep out of bed, and then the death would not catch them so easily."

"Yes. Yes. I suppose that is true," unreadily assented the Sheep, and left very shortly after in case the Tailor might add another to his already great load of fears.

Ansty's interest was awakened when the clay began to take form. Then she was, in the beginning, afraid of it. She removed her cream pans from the Room to a cupboard under the stairs. Whatever curse may fall upon the place as the result of this latest prank of "himself", the cream must be preserved from harm at all costs.

But, in spite of her fear, she could not resist a sally. From the safe distance of the doorway she watched the operation once or twice. "Look at my divil! You'd think to look at him and the mug of him that he was a statoo in a chapel." Familiarity with the sight of the "image" gradually made her contemptuous.

Cork Echo did not like the idea at all. In the beginning it was mysterious to him, and he could not understand it. Then, when the "image" was taking form, it roused all his religious scruples.

"It isn't right, Tailor. It isn't right, I tell you. It's a graven image and it is against the commandments. The church is against it, and all the popes."

"Yerra, what harm! What harm can there be in a head? Didn't you make a couple of small lads, whole and entire, body, legs, head and all, yourself, and you talk about an ould head."

Dan Bedam almost scratched his own head off in puzzlement at it. He could not understand it at all.

"Bedam, Tailor, I hear that you are having a new head made."

"That's true enough, Dan. A brand-new head that will last a hundred years, made of bronze, the hardest substance there is. It won't be affected by the heat or the cold or the sun or the rain."

"Bedam, that's queer. I've never heard of the likes of that before."

"It's a new patent, Dan. They have got a new method of making people because the young people nowadays are failing at the job, and the population of the country is going down."

"Bedam, I didn't hear that."

"There are a lot of new wonders in the world nowadays, Dan. There's aeroplanes and cars and wireless, and now this new way of making people."

"Bedam, but I've heard it said that wonders will never cease."

"True for you, Dan. Wonders will never cease so long as women kiss donkeys."

Dan disappeared on one of his errands. After a while he came back to redden his pipe and to have another look at the Tailor's own head. He did not know that the "image" was in the other room.

"Bedam, I was thinking, Tailor, will you be able to use it? Will you be able to talk and smoke and see with it?"

"Thon amon dieul! What the hell do you think that I am having it made for? Do you think that I want to become a dummy? I tell you that when I have this head I will be a different man. You have often heard tell that you cannot put a young head on old shoulders. Well, this is what it is. I was thinking of having it done the other way at first. Of having a new body fitted to my old head, but the expense for the bronze was too much, so I am starting with the head first. Then I thought that the new brains would not be so good as the old ones. Then I thought that the old ones had done a power of thinking in their time and it would be better after all to make a start with the head."

Dan was lost in wonderment for a while.

"Bedam, but Seamus Murphy must be a clever man."

"Clever! I should think he is. He's as good as Daniel O'Connell and Owen Roe put together. They were good enough in the old-fashioned way, but before he's finished he'll have the whole of Ireland populated again. It's a much quicker way than the way you had of going about the business, Dan."

"Bedam, it must me. I must tell herself about it tonight." Dan went back to his journeying with wonder and amazement.

The daily sessions continued with interest and much verbal assistance from the Tailor. He remembered a story about a man who made a statue – but that story will not bear repetition.

"I think that if you tighten your mouth, it would be better, Tailor;" suggested Seamus.

"True for you, Seamus. It's the loose mouth that does all the harm in the world. I remember a man by the name of—" And it was another quarter of an hour before he stopped talking and the mouth was tight enough for the work to proceed.

He had one tooth left in his head. It was a very large canine which was completely useless, but of which he was very proud. It even had a name. He referred to it always as "The Inchcape Rock".

"I tell you that that tooth has enjoyed itself. It was no fun in its day when it had all its companions. They were the boys for you. Many's the half-gallon of porter that has swirled around that, and many is the pig that it has made mincemeat of."

"I am going to tackle your hair now, Tailor."

"Fire away, Seamus, my boy. Fire away. I have forgotten how many there are of them, but they are all numbered, according to the Book. But one wrong here or there won't make any difference. The divil a bit."

Now and again Ansty peered into the room to see what progress was being made.

"Will you look at my ould shtal? Will you look at the puss on him? You'd think that he was all cream, sitting up there looking like a statoo in the chapel, and the divil doing nothing all the time but planning lies and the shtories."

"You'd better get yourself tidied up a bit," commanded the Tailor in the midst of one of her commentaries.

"Whyfor should I get tidied?" she asked with surprise.

"We'll have to go and see the priest when this is done," explained the Tailor.

"For what, you divil?"

"Thon amon dieul! don't be asking questions but do as you are told. We have to go and get married again. You were only married to the old head, and you will have to be married to the new head now, or we will be living in sin."

"Hould, you divil!"

The day for the plaster casting arrived. The Tailor discovered all manner of possibly useful things for the job in Cornucopia. When at last the job was done he complimented Seamus. "A damn neat job. It could not have been done better if I had done it myself."

The cast was trimmed and carried away for the metal casting. Then Seamus brought it back to Garrynapeaka and the whole valley was invited to the exhibition of "The Tailor's New Skull".

It was placed on the stand in the dim light of the Studio with a dark cloth behind it. The door was closed. The guests were assembled. The stout and the beer and the whiskey were opened, and all was expectancy.

The occasion was graced by the presence of the "Saint", another old friend of the Tailor's, whom Ansty calls "the biggest divil in Ireland – after himself", with a complete lack of reverence for the cloth. The "Saint" made a speech on the marvels of this new wonder, and opened the Studio door with a string, revealing "The Tailor's New Skull".

There was the rapt silence of wonder for a moment. Then Ansty, who was bored with the whole affair, and what seemed to her to be a quite unnecessary amount of fuss about nothing at all, and who had bustled and pushed through the crowd, ripped the silence asunder.

"How are the hens by ye, Johnny Mac?"

Ansty's inconsequential remark brought the assembly back to earth. The Sheep had been gazing, with eyes agog, first at the Tailor and then at the image, scarcely able to believe what he saw.

"It's devilish. It's devilish, I tell you, Tailor." He grunted assent with his own remark, and hastened away from the house with his drink only half finished.

Dan Bedam was stirred to expression.

"Bedam!" he gasped, "bedam, but ... do you know ... but it greatly resembles the Tailor!"

The Tailor himself hopped up to it and gave it a crack with his knuckles. "There you are. A fine head. There's a head will wear out several bodies, and it will break the jaws of any flea or midge that tries to bite it!"

"Look at him, will you? Look at my ould shtal," breaks in Ansty, seeing a chance of pricking the Tailor's latest balloon, "my ould devil of the two heads, and the one he has already is no use by him. It's another bottom he needs, for the one he has he's nearly worn out, sitting on it in the corner all day long, and shmoking and planning lies."

"Wouldn't you like a bust of yourself done, Mrs Buckley?" asks the "Saint" sweetly, almost certain of the reply. "A bust of you and the Tailor would make a grand show together."

"Busht! Busht!" Ansty snorts with contempt. "If you want a match for that ould devil you can make a busht of my backside!"

It was a great night. The drink flowed and the tongues were loosened. The Tailor sang and everyone sang and soon the "busht" was forgotten. But the Tailor keeps in touch with it still. He has cuttings from the papers relating to it, and he follows it round from exhibition to exhibition in the newspapers.

Nor has Ansty forgotten. Now and again she contemplates

the Tailor for a moment or two and wonders, and then expresses her thoughts. "And to think that Seamus made a busht of that ould devil as though he was a saint in a church. The man must be half cracked. As cracked as himself. Glory be! and to think that he wouldn't settle the leak in the chimney for me, and he with the good mortar and plaster, making a 'busht'."

Chapter Fifteen

The Tailor is sitting on Cornucopia reading a newspaper that someone has left for him or that has come wrapped round something from the shop. He would never think of buying a paper, even if he could. They do not extend to that importance in his scheme of things.

"Is there any news in the paper?" you ask. He puts down the paper eagerly at the interruption and smiles.

"The divil a bit – except a bit here I see at the back end of it," he adds, after a moment's pause, "where I see how a corncrake raped a butterfly in the county of Limerick and they are thinking of giving him a scholarship for it. Yerra! did any man ever see any news in a newspaper that mattered at all? Did I ever see what sort of a calf the cow would have or how the potatoes are doing?

"People are mad to be reading newspapers, and I don't know why, for all that they do is to soften a man's brain so that he can't think for himself. They are as bad as 'the fags', which thin a man's blood to water, so that he falls into bad health. I'll tell you of a thing which happened years ago.

"There was a man who had a farm of land and there were two sons at home working with him. The three of them were saving the hay, and the weather came on pretty bad and they were hard put to it.

"Well, by the hokey, in the middle of the day didn't one of the sons leave the field, and go into the house, and was not coming out again after a long while.

"The father sent the second son in to see what could be the matter, and he found the brother sitting by the fire reading the paper.

"'My father wants to know what is the matter with you,' he asked, 'that you are not coming to the work in the meadow.'

"'Tell him,' said the other fellow, 'that there is war in Sudan.'

"The brother went back and told the father.

"'The divil mend him and his "war in Sudan",' said the father. 'Go back and tell him that the real news is that the hay is rotting in the fields! The paper he is reading must be out of date.'"

107

That story sums up his own attitude towards newspapers. The most important news is the news nearest home. Its value and interest increase according to its proximity. We are not all Ministers of State, and anyway we never hear about such matters until they have happened. Newspapers are sources of amusement. They are trigger-springs to talk and imagination, rather than sources of information about anything that really matters. Human beings matter more than news. The warm sound of a human voice more than the strident shriek of a headline.

"Newspapers are like Old Moore's Almanac," suggested the Tailor upon another occasion. "Did you ever see Old Moore's Almanac? Well, it tells all the things that are going to happen in a kind of way. Most things do happen, anyway, if you wait long enough for them, only Old Moore doesn't tell you how long you will have to wait.

"When Old Moore was dying, his son came to him and asked of him the secret of how to write it, for it seemed to him an easy way of making money and he thought that he may as well carry on the business.

" 'The divil a secret,' said Old Moore. 'Write anything you like but one thing. Never say that there'll be snow in August.' "

When the Tailor does read a newspaper, he uses it. He will dig out an obscure paragraph which has some relationship to a remembrance or experience of his own, and he will completely ignore the headlines. In another sense, too, he makes use of newspapers. You can clean the chimney of the oil lamp with them. You can make spills from them with which to light your pipe.

"It seems to me," said the Tailor one day, between the puffs, "that Dev's party is after failing. The Irish Press" (de Valera's party organ) "doesn't light so well as it used to do. I must change my politics."

Kindly people give him magazines and books. Page by page they are torn asunder and are judged, not by their contents, but by their inflammability. "So-and-so brought me in a book the other night. It was very poor. The paper would hardly burn for you at all."

Yet, though he is contemptuous of the printed word, he has, in his earlier days, learnt quite a lot from books. He is familiar with most of the Irish poets and the Irish and the Greek mythology. But while there is life, and the change of season, and the change of weather, and the road runs through Garry-napeaka, the Tailor has no time for books.

"Have you ever thought of writing a book yourself, Tailor?"

"Writing a book? Yerra, manalive, I've thought of many

more things than that, but somehow I have not had the time. But if I did write a book I would give all the instruction of the old time. I would put things before the present generation and show them what the world was, and what the world is, and show them the length of their noses before their faces.

"By the mockstick of war! There is a deal of difference between the world as it was then and the world as it is today. I have known a man who was earning three shillings a week who was able to buy a farm of land, and did buy a farm of land, because his money was not spent in luxury and debauchery as it is nowadays.

"Did you ever see a book called *The Book of Knowledge*? It was that which partly turned me away from the idee. It was Cork Echo who first saw the advertisement, and it was he who told the others and persuaded them all to put their money together and to buy it. I was against the business from the beginning, for I did not see how there could be anything printed in a book that could ever be of any use to any man. The only knowledge that is any use or any value to a man is that which he learns himself by living.

"But the rest of them were soon clean mad for it. They thought that if only they had it they could sit on their backsides for the rest of their lives, and the world would come to them, and they would be the whole push. Yerra, they thought that they would be better than anything that was ever in a circus.

"Well, I joined in to make the money up, and Cork Echo wrote to the address in London where they had the book and told them to send it along, and he sent them earnest money, and told them that we would send the rest when we had the book got.

"After a week or two they wrote to him and told him that the book was waiting for him at Macroom station and he must come in for it with a horse and cart, and that there was five pounds to pay, and that he would not get the book until he paid the money.

"There was a big fair in Macroom a couple of days later, and happen Cork Echo himself was going in with a couple of fat pigs, so he said that he would have a look at the book as well, and see was it worth the money.

"He went along to the station, and right enough there was a case for him, a bloody great case. He knew the man of the station, a decent man he was too. He had a near relation to him by marriage. He told him his business, and the man agreed that you did not want to be spending all that money without seeing what you were getting, so they opened the case and there were dozens of books inside.

"The first one was all about Architecture and Archaeology.

They put that one back. That was no damned use at all. The second one was about 'Bogwrappy' and Botany, and they pitched that to hell. So they opened three or four, but they both said that you would need a dictionary to read the titles let alone what was inside them. Cork Echo said that the only use he could see for them was to build a fence to a field, and he already had enough stones in his fields to fence all the fields in Ireland.

"The man of the station thought that it would be a great waste of money to spend five pounds on a lot of books with queer titles like that, and maybe some of them were the works of the devil, and you couldn't tell what might happen if you read them. You might be changed into a goat, whereas you did know where you were if you spent the money on porter.

"So they nailed the case up again and sent it back to London, but the people in London wrote several letters wanting to be paid for it. But we devised a plan and wrote back to them and told them that, if they really knew so much as to be able to write a book called the book of knowledge, they ought to have known that we were not going to buy it, and not to be wasting any more time writing. That settled them and we heard no more from them.

"Book of Knowledge! Book of Knowledge!

"I tell you that the old people had more knowledge than ever went into any book. Didn't they know all that was going to happen, and didn't they put it all into a wise and witty way in the Prophecies? They were the boys who had the knowledge."

The academic calm is broken by the entry of Ansty, bearing an armful of sticks, which she hurls down in the middle of the floor.

"I suppose that you were too busy talking about your book of knowledge to know that the fire is nearly out?" she asks.

The sarcasm passes the Tailor by.

"Shift yourself, you divil. Sitting there like an ould sow. Put a sod of turf behind the fire and a stick on it, and hang the kettle. It's time for the tea."

The Tailor changes from the role of Minerva to that of Vesta, and soon has the fire blazing, and the kettle singing. He takes up the thread of his discourse again.

"I remembered last night, after you had gone, a piece I had out of the paper, and all the morning I was looking for it, but, the divil mend it, I can't find it anywhere. Herself does be 'tidying'; and I declare to God but you can never find a thing when she has done 'tidying'.

"But I remember the most of it. It was a bit about a German doctor in America, who was in a hole thirty-five feet deep in the ground, and he was weighing the earth. There was a picture of him with a damn fine 'brusher' (beard). Oh! a neat brusher entirely."

"Thirty-five feet deep! Glory be!" punctuates Ansty, as she picks away at a piece of bread.

"That was six months ago, and he had a good piece of it done then. He must be nearly finishing it now."

"Weighing the earth! The Lord save us!"

You visualize Ansty's visualization of him weighing the earth on a grocer's balance. She is soon bored with it, however. It is too much of a strain upon the imagination. She develops an unharmonious duet.

"Did you see the great shtal of a beggar that walked up the road today?"

"That wasn't all he was doing, however—"

"You may say that I gave him a relement—"

"—he was a queer artist altogether—"

"—My shtal walked into me and said how he was looking for work, and I told him to go to Mick Lucey—"

"—he was also making a kind of a clock—"

"—but, no, he would not go there—"

"—You gave it so many turns a day—"

"—So I told him to go to Sweeney's, but that wouldn't do him either—"

"—and it keeps the daylight so that it would be day inside the house when it would be night outside—"

"—so I told him that I might as well employ him myself, and he asked me what work I had for him—"

"—that's a powerful patent, I can tell you—"

"—and I told him he—"

"—Marvellous are the works of man, as the man said, stepping over the baby—"

"—could scratch my bottom—"

Everyone, actors and audience, is exhausted after this. There is a moment's breathing space.

"Stepping over the baby! Wisha! How well you were there to see him! Get up and see where the cow is. Johnny Con's cows are easht, and she'll be fighting with them."

"The divil fire you and your cow. If she is in she ought to be out. If she is out she ought to be in. If she is east she ought to be west. Never was any man, since the creation of the world, bothered so much as I am with you and your cow."

"When I was in the city of Cork and in Dublin and in Scotland I saw everything that was to be seen. I went to circuses and concerts and the opera, and they were all good enough in their way, but, do you know, that the best sport that I ever had was around this fire.

"People do be thinking that the life in the country is dull, and they are wrong. If the man knows the place where he is, and takes an interest in the place where he is, he can never be dull. If a man knows the people about him, as you do come to know them after years, he can never be dull at his own fireside. He won't have the time for reading books and listening to the wireless. Those are only a poor class of entertainment to a man compared with living people.

"People have always resorted to this house. Before my time, when Ansty's father was alive, it was a great house of resort, and it still is. There'd be card-playing and dancing and singing and talking and stories and planning. There's a lot of fun gone up that chimney with the smoke – and very little harm.

"I suppose that you don't remember 'Lollipopus'? That would be before your time, but you would not know it anyway by that name, for it was myself gave it that name.

"Years ago there would be some of them who resorted here would be mad for the news in the papers. The most of them were poor scholars and they would get me to read the paper to them. It saved time too.

"Well, at this time they were making a lot of fuss about a star which had gone on fire. You would see it yourself tearing about the sky with flames and smoke pouring out of it.

"The papers called it a comet – 'Healy's comet'. But how the hell could it belong to Healy, or to any man, come to that? It was a lot of damned nonsense calling it 'Healy's comet'. You might as well say that the sun belonged to Dan Bedam.

"So I christened it, and the name I put on it was 'Lollipopus', which was a good enough name for it. It did not mean anything else, and a name is only to know a thing by.

"Everybody was very interested in Lollipopus, and every night there would be a lot about it. One day there was a bit in the paper where an astronomer said that, if it touched the earth, it would burn the earth up. And the way that it was tearing about like a bull you couldn't tell what it would do next.

"We talked about this for a while, and some of them got afraid. Then we talked about other things, and then a bit of an argument broke out. There's a hill up there beyond Derreenowen, called Coolclogh, and at that time it held a fright of cover on it of old furze and heather and fern.

"Cork Echo had heifers out on the mountain and he was mad to burn the top of Coolclogh, lest his heifers got lost in it, for there were some fierce holes in it as well, under the cover. But the mountain was common land, held by all the people at

Derreenowen, neighbours of Cork Echo, and because Cork Echo wanted to burn it no one else would agree to burn it.

"Anyway, he was always mad to be burning, and still is. They would not take him seriously and thought that his heifers was only an old excuse. He would spend all night up with a fire he had started. There was no sense or meaning to half the fires he started. I told him once that he must have taken out his papers to the devil, and be serving his apprenticeship to hell.

"After a while the argument over Coolclogh broke down and we started some other business. When that was over, the company broke up. As they were going out they fell to talking again about Lollipopus, and I said we had better say 'Good-bye' to each other in case we were burnt alive in our sleep, for I had been thinking.

"Cork Echo stayed behind. He would not walk back with the others. When they had gone the two of us were sitting by the fire smoking for a piece. Then I said to him:

" 'Wouldn't it be great aise to you if Coolclogh was burnt?'

" 'It would,' said he, 'the greatest aise in the world.'

" 'Have you tried praying for it to be burned?' I asked then, for he was always a religious class of man.

" 'I have,' said he. 'I've pestered every saint that I have ever heard of for it to be burned.'

" 'Do you know,' said I, 'but I think that your prayers are in the way of being answered.'

" 'You don't say so! Now how could that be? Do you see a fire?'

" 'Fire be damned. Didn't you hear the bit about Lollipopus tonight? Don't you see that that is the answer to your prayers?'

" 'How the hell could it be? What has that to do with it?' The man was a bit backward.

" 'Thon amon dieul! Haven't you any brains at all, man? Think. Use them. If Lollipopus touches the earth doesn't this astronomer say that the earth will be burned?'

" 'Yes. He said that right enough.'

" 'Well, if it touches Coolclogh, won't that be burned?'

" 'Yes. I suppose it would. But how is it going to touch Coolclogh? I don't see that at all.'

" 'That's the worst of you religious people. You just want to get down on your knees and say prayers and leave it at that. You want to leave all the work to someone else. Haven't you ever heard that the Lord helps those who help themselves? Don't you see that Lollipopus is your boy? Do you mean to say that you are so blind that you don't see that it is the answer to your prayers?'

"The man was stupid, and it took me a long time to knock

sense into his head, but at last I did manage to make the plan clear to him.

"He was to go home, and when the place was quiet, out in the small hours of the morning, he was to go up to Coolclogh and fire it. It was fine and dry and there was a right breeze blowing, and it would not be long in getting its head. Then he was to come down and take his clothes off and change into his night-shirt, and when the fire was well alight, to go bawling and shrieking round the neighbours' houses in Derreenowen.

" 'Lollipopus has touched the earth! Lollipopus has touched the earth! We'll all be burned alive! Get down on your knees and say your prayers! The end of the world has come!'

"Then he was to get them all together saying the Rosary and keep one eye on the fire to see that it was doing well enough, so that it could not be beaten out. I'd fix the other end of the business.

"Well, when he had the plan into his head he got scruples. God give me patience with such people! It is a sort of disease religious people get. I've never had it myself, but I have seen a number of people were driven dotty by it. They think that everything they do is a sin. I don't know why they don't go and drown themselves. They must have the priests driven crazy with it.

" 'But it wouldn't be right!' said he.

" 'Right!' said I. 'The divil break your legs with your "it wouldn't be right". Haven't you been praying for it to happen? And now you have a miracle handed out to you – the greatest opportunity any man ever had since the beginning of the world, and you say "it wouldn't be right"! Have you no sense at all, man?'

"He said he had sense, but his conscience was troubling him.

" 'To hell with your conscience! If I was the Almighty, I'd lose patience with you people who pester the life out of me with your prayers. You're like a pack of tom-cats, just making a noise because you can think of nothing else to do. Do you expect the Almighty to come down with a box of matches and set fire to Coolclogh Himself? Do you think that He has nothing better to do with His time than that? He answers your prayers. He puts opportunity in your way, and you are too blind and stupid to see it. Thon amon dieul! I've almost lost patience with you myself.'

"Then he agreed, and then he thought it was not right again. He'd be deceiving people and they might find out that he did it. No. It would not be right.

" 'Right! Right! The divil fire you and your "right". It will be the best thing that you ever did. If you get to heaven at all this is the greatest chance you will ever get. Won't you be getting Jerry the Rover down on his knees, with the fear of God in his heart for the first time for years? Haven't you often said yourself that he is a danger and a disgrace to the parish? Won't you be doing more than any priest or missioner in Ireland has ever been able to do with him?'

"He began to see a bit of sense at this, so I struck while the hook was in him.

"'Do you know,' I went on, 'I wouldn't be a bit surprised if they didn't make you a saint for this or perhaps a holy martyr.'

"That put salt on his tail and he went off, after I had repeated the plan to him and seen that he had it right, as pleased as could be with himself, imagining himself a saint along with Saint Patrick and the rest of them.

"He carried out the plan just as I told him. He fired Coolclogh and went bawling round Derreenowen in his night-shirt, and he got Jerry the Rover down on his knees, with the rest of them, saying the Rosary and the fear of God in them, and Coolclogh was burned as bare as the top of a bald man's head.

"All the following day there was talk but of the wonder of Lollipopus, and the miraculous escape they all had, and how it was due to Cork Echo waking them all up and getting them to say the Rosary in time. I praised him, and said that I always did think that there was a touch of the saint about him, and the people went on talking.

"Two nights later I read them the paper as usual, and I read them a bit that wasn't in the paper at all. I learned it by rote, and I have it still.

"'Healy's comet touches mountain in West Cork. Disaster averted by one man.

"'In the early hours of yesterday morning when everyone was asleep Healy's comet touched the top of Coolclogh, one of the highest mountains in West Cork. The top of the mountain was fired, and the fire was spreading rapidly down the side of the mountain to Derreenowen, where a number of families were sleeping, innocent of the great danger that was upon them.

"'One man, however, who was saying his prayers before going to bed, saw the awful fire and rushed round to his neighbours with not a stitch on him but his night-shirt through the bitterly cold night, and called them all.

"'He led them in saying the Rosary, so that the fire was turned back by a miracle and all lives were saved, and the earth was saved from destruction, as prophesied by the most famous astronomer in the world. The brave act of this man has been brought to the notice of the bishop, who has sent the news to the Pope in Rome.'

"Do you know that Cork Echo is one of the stupidest men that ever walked? Do you know that he complained the following day that he had caught a cold by being out in his night-shirt?

"'The divil break your legs,' said I to him. 'You have had your prayers answered. You have got what you wanted done for years. You have worked a miracle, and you are well on the way to being made a saint, and you grumble because you have caught a cold! I declare to God but the Almighty has more patience than I gave Him credit for!'

"I tell you, those were the airy times and those were the airy people. But all that happened a long time ago. It could be thirty years ago the next holy day in August—"

"Thirty years ago!" spat Ansty, who had sat through the story without a sound. "Thirty years ago! Is it taking leave of your senses that you are with your – thirty years ago?"

The Tailor is a little startled by the unexpected interruption, but after a moment he recovers his balance and continues, "—thirty years ago on the next holy day in August."

"I tell you it is not!" interrupted Ansty again.

"Thon amon dieul!" answered the Tailor, with rising anger. "As sure as there is a tail on a cat it was thirty years ago."

"It's clean mad you are with your thirty years ago."

There was a silent pause while the Tailor reflected. Then he started in again, like a leading counsel laying a complicated trap.

"Wasn't it thirty years ago that Jack the Ram was married?"

"Am Bostha! if it was, what has that to do with it at all?"

"Wasn't that the year that I sold the black heifer calf in Bantry fair? Wasn't that the year that Timmy Johnny went to America? Wasn't that the year—?"

"Listen to him, will you, with his 'wasn't that the year'. You'd think it was saying his beads he was."

The Tailor returned to the defence with a new tack.

"How old is Denny Mary Jamesy? Wasn't he thirty-one years last Christmas, and wasn't his father married to the Loughra woman the year before at the same time as the 'Redbreast'? . . . Well, so!"

"Leave me alone with him! Didn't the Loughra woman marry the Yank? Wasn't she a first cousin to Mary John the Pub? And she only had the two girls, and one of them went away to America, and the other married Jim – Jimmy Faddy?"

"She was not, I tell you. There was no relation at all unless it was on her mother's side, for her mother was a Kerry woman from near to Morley's Bridge, and there may have been a relationship far out but no more. Her father was a Leary of Carrigdubh. Didn't I know him as well as I know you? Wasn't it many the piece of a night that we spent together card-playing? Wasn't his sister married over in America to Paddy Pat Buie, and haven't I a relation myself to him, for the Pat Buies were near related to my brother's wife's people. Thon amon dieul, woman! Talk sense."

"Talk sense! Listen to who's telling me to 'talk sense'. I tell you, you're half cracked!"

"Have it so. There is no one thinks themselves so sound in the head as the mad people."

While the Tailor carelessly enjoys his moment of victory, Ansty puzzles and returns to the attack.

"Didn't the 'Redbreast' marry the daughter of Long John? And hasn't Johnny Mary Jamesy been the age of the pension since last October and—"

"Hould your whist, woman. I tell you you haven't a bit of the head. You do get up too early in the morning, worrying about the cow. I am sorry for you."

"Sorry me eye! I tell you it was so."

There is a pause. The Tailor becomes aware of his audience again, and takes up the lost thread.

"—that happened about nineteen hundred and ten!"

He has won the last round.

"Nineteen hundred and ten!" echoes Ansty without comprehension. "Glory be! Nineteen hundred and ten! Fancy that!"

Chapter Sixteen

It is related of Socrates that on the occasion of a triumphal procession he stood in the street as a spectator. All the riches of the then-known earth, all the desired things of life were carried past him in the procession. When it was all over, it is told that he said, "What a rich man am I. What few things there are in this world I desire."

The Tailor of Garrynapeaka does not express his similar thoughts in words. He expresses them in his life. The true judgment of a man is not to be made on what a man says, but on how he lives. The Tailor lives richly, and is rich. There are few things he desires or even needs out of this world more than he has.

(The resemblance to Socrates goes further. Socrates had Xanthippe to tether him to earth. The Tailor has Ansty to prick the balloon of his imagination, and keep him from soaring too high from reality.)

There is much to be learnt in Garrynapeaka. Much more of the reality of living than the schools and the universities teach. It holds within it in essence all that we can ever hope to get out of living.

"There was a man telling me," started the Tailor, "of Henry Ford, who makes the motor-cars, and how he had an income of twenty million pounds a year. I reckoned that out, and do you know what it means?"

"Twenty million pounds a year! The Lord save us!"

"It means that he could give over six pounds every year to every man, woman and child in Ireland!"

"Six pounds every year? To everyone in Ireland? Thon amon dieul! He must be a wealthy man. Six pounds every year! He must have the grass of forty cows – at least," ponders Ansty.

"There is another man in England who makes motors, and I was reading a bit about him in the paper the other day. Do you know that he says that his money is such a worry to him he can't sleep at night!"

"Why doesn't he send some of it to me?" asks Ansty. "I'd drive the divil of a shpree on it. Six pounds. Glory be, you could have a grand shpree on that."

"Do you know, when you come to think of it," continues the Tailor, ignoring the remarks from the gallery, "it is no wonder that the world is clean daft. People think that those men are rich. I tell you that they are not. I tell you that they are about the poorest men for living that the world has ever known. There is many a beggar, walking the lanes of Ireland, has a much better life than either of those. There are two men with all that money, and there are thousands who have not got a bite to eat and no means of getting it. I tell you the world has gone to alabastery, and it's no wonder that there is a war. Not that a war will do anyone any good. What is needed is that people start thinking for themselves, and thinking rightly, and begin to see the length of their noses before their faces."

"Six pounds! Glory be. All the whiskey you could get for six pounds. Ring a dora!"

"No man can sleep in more than one bed at a time, nor eat two meals at a time, nor have more than twenty-four hours in the day— no matter how much money he has. But people won't see the sense of that. They think of money alone, and don't seem to realize that money was never a bit of use to a man until he got rid of it."

In the daily life and the economics of Garrynapeaka you will see, put into practice, what the Tailor is sometimes roused to preach.

There is plain, simple, satisfying and health-giving food. There is fresh milk and butter, thick milk and buttermilk. There are potatoes and cabbage and onions in the garden. There are fresh eggs. There is oatmeal and home-made soda cake. There is salt ling and bacon, hanging from the rafters . . . "and God, who made good laughter, has seen that it is good."

There is sweet water in the spring well. There is the shelter of a roof, and the comfort of a glowing turf fire. There is fresh air and a wide and varying view. There are all the human contacts of the place.

What more could riches provide? Only an elaboration of these things. It could change the salt ling to a dish with a French name, but it could not provide the zestful appetite with which the Tailor tackles it. It could provide more luxurious furniture, but then one would have to change to fit the furniture. When the Tailor starts his "planning", you forget the minor discomfort of the furniture. You might have one without the other. Take first things, human things, first, and let the rest come after.

Yesterday the Tailor bought a pig in the fair and had it killed and cleaned. It was delivered to him a while ago and dumped on

119

the settle, to the side of the Tailor seated on Cornucopia. He has been ranging over other topics, but again and again comes back to the pig. He turns round to look at it. His eyes gleam. He gives it a resounding smack on the rump. "Thon amon dieul! But there's months of grand eating in that. Do you know, I think that you and I," he continues, addressing the carcass of the pig, "will agree greatly with each other, if you have as much of a mind for me as I have for you.

"I reckoned up how much that pig cost me as meat," he went on. "When you take in a few pence for the salt, it will work out at about twopence-farthing a pound. That is cheap living. You would pay at least one shilling and sixpence for the cheaper parts of that if you were to buy it in a town."

It will be cut up and salted in a barrel, and when "saved" it will be hung from the rafters to smoke. As it is required, a piece will be taken down, and the salt boiled from it, and then the Tailor, who does most of the cooking, will make "a potash" of it in the bastable or iron pot in which all the cooking is done.

The rest of the economy of Garrynapeaka is on the same standard. The soda bread is made at home, in the bastable, with buttermilk and bread soda. Now and again Ansty will allow one of her precious ducks or hens to be eaten. The Tailor sometimes develops a passion for beef, and will get someone to bring out a few pounds of it from Macroom or Bantry.

The cottage is one of the many built under the Labourers' Cottage Act of 1880. For its four rooms and outhouses and its acre of mountain land the Tailor pays, with rates, four pounds five shillings a year. He pays another few shillings a year for the right to cut turf from a neighbouring farmer's bog.

Ansty sells butter and eggs at the local shop, and buys tea, sugar, soap, candles, oil, oatmeal and flour by the half sack. Clothes cost little. The arts of the fashion creators get short shrift in Garrynapeaka. Clothes are utilitarian. A suit is patched until almost all trace of its original cloth has gone. You do not need a morning suit to tend cattle or walk through the mountains.

Ansty has new clothes, which she has never worn, and never will wear. On Sundays and holy days she dresses herself neatly, and wears over all the West Cork hooded cloak, which will, by the excellence of its material, outlast her lifetime.

Most of the furnishings of the house are as old as the house itself. Some of them are much older. There are chairs, a settle, a bed, tables and a dresser of ware. There are wooden tubs and "keillers" and buckets. What else does a house need?

The light of the oil lamp and the soft firelight are enough for the winter nights. There is little reading of books. There are the real human stories of the day to be told by the fireside.

The acre of land provides potatoes, cabbage, oats, hay and grazing for the cow. The oats are not threshed, but stacked and fed to the cow during the winter. Neighbouring farmers do the bit of tilling which is necessary, in exchange for a few days' help from the Tailor's son, who also cuts and draws home the turf from the bog.

Ansty, who is an excellent manager, sells butter and eggs and chickens. The Tailor has an old age pension of ten shillings a week. Ansty is a few years yet from "the age of the pension". They are "passing rich on twenty-six pounds a year".

"The dairy herd", the single black cow, is the hub of the household. To a stranger it seems to loom too large altogether in the scheme of things. It is Ansty's chief preoccupation of the day. Her days start with the cow, and only when it is safely housed for the night does she relax at all. It is about the only part of the domestic procedure that the Tailor himself takes at all seriously.

Let the Tailor explain why himself. It happened one day, when someone had come to the conclusion that many people have come to before, but have been proved to be wrong, and have "had Salamanca knocked out of their ignorance".

The Tailor was sitting on the ditch, minding the "dairy herd" by volleying abuse at Carlo and goading him to "talk to it" in a language it could better understand than even the Tailor's abuse.

"Do you know, Tailor, if I had Garrynapeaka, the first thing that I would do would be to get rid of that cow or any cow."

"Then the first thing you would do would be to show the height of your stupidity. You might as well go and drown yourself, for you would be a poor man without a cow," he replied, speaking *ex cathedra*.

"Is that a bit of vanity, or is it because the cow is a hobby? Surely you don't really need a cow? I have heard of the pig as 'the gentleman who pays the rent', but I don't see the justification for having a cow – unless, of course, you just honestly like having a cow."

"Thon amon dieul! I have often said that a man can learn something fresh every day, and come upon a new wonder between getting up in the morning and going to bed again at night. And it is true. Today I have met the stupidest man in the world.

"The pig! The pig!" he continued in scorn. "Yerra, manalive, the pig is only a bank, but the cow is the hub of the household. You couldn't think of having a pig unless you kept a cow first. If you were to come here you would first have to get a wife, and then a cow. And the first thing you would have to look for in the

121

wife would be if she was a good milker. You might get the cow as dowry with the wife, and you could not do better, unless there was a bit of money as well. If you had the cow, you could live without the wife, but if you had not the cow you would not be able to live at all."

"I still think that keeping a cow would be an unnecessary luxury as well as an unnecessary nuisance," persisted the ignoramus.

"And I still think that you have an unnecessary amount of head for the small use you do be making of it," retaliated the Tailor. "Now listen to me, and let me put some wisdom into you for a change.

"That cow cost me eight pounds in Bantry fair. She is a good cow, and she is worth more now than I paid for her.

"She provides us with milk. Milk to drink and 'colouring' for the tea. Then she provides us with the thick milk and with the buttermilk. How could you eat the potatoes without the thick milk; and how could you bake the cake without the buttermilk; and how could you get through the heat of the summer without the buttermilk – the best drink a man ever had – almost! That's the first splink of sense for you to learn.

"But that's not the end of the lesson. Not by a deal. Next comes the butter. For at least five months of the year she provides, over our own needs, about seven pounds of butter during the week. Sometimes it goes up to nine or ten pounds. 'Herself' sells that at about a shilling a pound. You can call that thirty shillings a month.

"She will 'go to dairy' once a year. That costs half a crown for 'the pusher' (the bull). The calf she will have will sell for thirty shillings, and that is cheap, for I sell her to a neighbour, who will give me a load of litter for her as well.

"She costs something to feed. Little enough. Not near so much as some people who cost a damned sight more and do a damned sight less. She has cabbage and oats and hay and grazing from the land. I have to buy a bit more hay and a bit of meal. That comes to about thirty shillings for the four months of the winter.

"Now we will go back to the producing end again. She helps provide the bread. If we were to buy bread, it would cost us near a shilling a day. That is eighteen pounds and five shillings in the year. But we are not so stupid as that. We buy flour, costing three pounds for the year, and make the soda cake with the buttermilk, and save fifteen pounds a year, and have something fit to eat, and our health along with that.

"Now we come to the potatoes and the cabbage. She helps to produce those as well. Potatoes and cabbage need manure, and

122

there is little of it to be bought in this part of the country. The land needs all that you can give it. It is as rare as sense in the cities, and, like it, it can't be bought.

"Land is useless without it. It is the cow who produces it, and so she helps to provide the potatoes and the cabbage. The divil a bit but the cow is a miracle entirely, so that a man could scarcely live without her. It would be like trying to hang your hat upon a rainbow, as to be trying to live without a cow.

"When she has done all this good work, it is then that you might start thinking about a pig. From what is left of her milk you could help fatten a pig, invest the surplus of her in the bank. I have done the same thing often enough myself; but you could not start to think of doing it until you had the cow.

"Now do you see why your notion of trying to live without a cow would be the height of madness?"

"Yes. But I still think that most people in England in your position would not keep a cow."

"England," snorts the Tailor. "England! It is just that which makes them what they are. They start off without a splink of sense. They sell honey in order to buy sweets, and they come here to learn their lessons. But this was ever known as the Island of Scholars."

A storm breaks the peace of Garrynapeaka. Ansty rushes on the scene, hair awry, and herself almost speechless, but only almost.

"Thon amon dieul! The divil break your legs! What good are you at all! Sitting there on your backside, talking, and the cow amongst the cabbages, and for the second time this week. The divil fire you, and the cow, and the cabbages."

The cow looks up from her munching and estimates the distance between herself and Ansty, and returns to her lopping of the cabbages. Ansty herself is torn between the two immediate needs – to bring the Tailor to book, and to check the ravages of the cow. The Tailor suddenly discovers that his pipe is not drawing as well as it should, and becomes deeply interested in poking it.

"Sitting there like a budogue or the pope himself and talking. Nothing but the talking. You may as well stay in the bed all the day for all the good you are about the place. God give me patience." So Ansty continues, while the cow continues to eat the cabbage. The storm passes over the Tailor's head. The pipe is much more important. Then Carlo gets a rough dash of Ansty's tongue, and replies with barks which stir the cow. It takes its last lop of the cabbage and leisurely moves away, before Ansty rounds it up, and takes it out of harm's way and the Tailor's way.

123

Peace returns to the acre. The Tailor lights his pipe again. Now it draws smoothly, and he has a job well done.

"There was a man long ago," he says, "by the name of Jim O'Driscoll, who was married to a woman by the name of MacCarthy, Mary MacCarthy.

"They had but a small way of living; a small farm and a big family. At that time people were after getting a bit enlightened, and they were having the tea for breakfast.

"James was smoking the tobacco. He would smoke sixpence worth in the week. It was threepence an ounce in those days. One night as they were sitting by the fire, and James smoking, he said, 'I am out of the tobacco. When the scholars are going to school in the morning, tell them to bring me a bit on their way home.'

" 'Well, James,' said Mary to him, 'you are smoking the tobacco, and we are drinking the tea every morning. We will have to give up either the tea or the tobacco. The expense is coming too heavy.'

" 'Very well,' said he, 'that is good enough. I will give up smoking the tobacco. We are both drinking the tea.'

"Happen very well. They went into a fair and good agreement. He gave up smoking the tobacco, and he remained that way with her for a month. He used to go to bed along with her, and used to have no more to do with her. He went on to a religious probation.

"After a month a beggarman walked into him, who used to stop with him, by the name of Paddy the Traveller. Paddy used to smoke, and before they went to bed himself and James were talking by the two sides of the fire. The wife had gone to bed, but could hear all that was said, and did hear all that was said.

"Paddy the Traveller said to James, after a while, 'I don't see you smoking. Maybe it is that you are out of the tobacco?'

" 'No,' replied James, 'it is not that at all, but it is how I broke my pipe.'

" 'Blast it, man,' said Paddy then to him, 'why didn't you say it all along? Have a smoke of this.' He handed him the pipe, and they smoked, and they talked for a while, and after that they went to bed. Mary, the wife, turned at him then, and he turned to her, and he made up for his month's religious probation, and she got her conjugal rights again.

"The following day when he came in to his dinner there were two ounces of tobacco and a new pipe on the shelf before him, and she never afterwards stopped him smoking.

"I tell you that he was the smart man for the settling of disputes, with never a harsh word said and no argument at all, but all settled to satisfaction in a good, quiet, respectable way."

Chapter Seventeen

When the work of the year is done, and the nights grow long, and there is time in plenty, the Tailor's nightly court grows in size. The settle will be full, and all the chairs will be occupied. There will be an overflow on to the stairs and the window-ledge.

The Tailor presides on Cornucopia. Ansty hovers in the background, still with the urge of work upon her, gradually subsiding in the rinsing of a cup, the hanging of a cloth, and the small, energyless jobs of the day's ending.

Every few minutes the door is opened and someone walks in.

"Thon amon dieul! How well you walked out? Yerra, we haven't seen you for this long time. We didn't know if you were dead or alive," greets Ansty.

"Welcome, Jamesy! Welcome, Johnny!" greets the Tailor. "How are things by ye?"

"Yerra," you hear Ansty reply in answer to an inquiry about herself, "not so good at all. I have a pain in my knee for the past couple of weeks."

The Tailor has heard her, and plays his part, and the evening opens.

"Beat it, woman. Beat it! It's how it is getting lazy, and will corrupt the other. You're saying too many prayers that's your trouble."

"Better for you say a few yourself," retorts Ansty, "and the priest coming to the house next week."

"Yerra, what harm if he come tonight? It would only be like the man who hadn't been to confession for fifteen years, and when the priest asked him what he had done since his last confession he said, 'Every God-damned blasted thing, Father, except suicide.' That was the shortest confession ever a man made."

"Listen to him. Always the shtories, out of the smoke, and the laughing, and then the complaining, and the complaining. Better for you stop the laughing, and put a sod of turf on the fire. Thon amon dieul! you'd think that we hadn't a sod of turf in the house."

Ansty hurls turf at the Tailor's feet, and he banks up the fire.

"She keeps you busy always, Tailor," remarks one of the company.

"Keeps me busy? Keeps me busy, indeed! Upon my word it is like something that happened in the city of Glasgow years ago. There were two women, and they both kept randy way-houses. One day one of them said to the other, 'How's business with you, Mrs MacGregor, these times?'

" 'We're terrible busy,' replied the other, 'terrible busy, entirely. Do you know that we are so busy that I have to take a turn myself now and again!' "

"How well you were there listening to her," punctuates Ansty. But she is tired of the argument, and turns aside to someone else.

"Did you hear how much Micky the Buck got for the sheep he sold today? A hundred and twenty pounds! He was here by us in the early part of the evening, and he was telling us how much he got for lambs, and how much for wethers, and how much for ewes. A hundred and twenty pounds! That for 'oo. He's the Micky who knows how to make the money, I tell you."

"Yes," agrees the Tailor, "he was sitting there opposite me, after having the tea drunk, and he was telling us about the day's transaction. 'And,' said he, when he had his story told, 'that's the tale of the day without a turn or a twist or a bend in it.' Without a turn or a twist or a bend in it! I declare to God that the hardest job anyone will ever have is to straighten the same Micky out for his wake. He won't even be able to lie straight when he is dead. The divil blast the lie is it."

Micky is not averse to selling another man's sheep unknown to him.

The Tailor continues: "This one looked down at his boots, which were poor enough, God knows. 'I expect that you will be able to buy yourself a new pair of shoes,' said she, 'out of the money?'

"I looked down at the shoes myself and then I looked up at Micky. 'Micky,' said I, 'I wouldn't be surprised if there wasn't the makings of another hundred and twenty pounds, and those shoes still – if only you use them rightly!' "

When the laughter fades, Ansty continues on the same theme. She challenges one of the company.

"You look as though you could do with a new pair of breeches yourself, Johnny Faddy."

"I could, God knows, Ansty, but where would I get the price of them? Times are bad. Times are bad. Perhaps you have an old pair yourself you could spare me?"

"Yerra, there's years of wear in those yet," asserts the Tailor. "It is only like the beggar and the song he used to sing." He starts in his quavering voice:

Oh! me breeches is broke and down me linen do hang,
And the girls, for sport, surround me all in a throng;
They treat me to beer, good cheer, and a glass of a dram,
And they'd follow me here if my beard grew seven yards long.
And they all do say, as meal they slash in me bag,
If that fellow were shaved he'd make a handsome young
man.

"Good man, Tailor. Good," comes the murmur of applause. A sly voice adds, "Not forgetting Jerry Mac's coat, Tailor!"

"Jerry Mac's coat? Jerry Mac's coat?" The Tailor puzzles for a moment, and then he laughs and laughs, and those who know the story join in the laughter. "By the mockstick of war!" said the Tailor, amidst the laughter, "but you may say that that was the coat that had a history, if ever a coat had."

"What is the history of it?" asks someone who is not in the know.

Everyone starts to tell the history of Jerry Mac's coat.

"It would be four years ago, wouldn't it, Tailor, that he brought it first?"

"—he wanted the Tailor to turn it for him—"

"—a damn good piece of stuff and well worth the turning—"

"—I said it was a simple enough job—"

"—What? The old frieze coat?—"

"—The very same—"

The Tailor takes the reins firmly into his hands, before the story runs away from him entirely.

"Herself was giving the place a 'rough dash' at the time with the whitewash, and I said that I would leave it till the place settled down, and I could do the job at my ease. I didn't want to be spoiling it with the lime on it. Well, I put it over the machine as a cover, for she puts more of the whitewash on the floor than on the walls, and I sort of forgot it for a while.

"Some time later, Jerry asked me how the coat was getting on, and that brought it back to mind again. 'I'll be starting on it tomorrow, and once it's started it won't be long,' I told him. 'Pon my soul! when tomorrow came, I found she had it taken and had put it under a hatching hen. 'Leave well alone,' said I. 'To remove it might upset the hen.' So it slipped from my mind for another piece.

"The next time I thought of it was when Cornucopia was wearing a bit thin, and the edges of it were catching my backside. I asked herself for an old bag, and she gave me the coat. Good enough! I put it on the top of the box, and it made a grand soft seat, and saved me a deal of suffering, and it kept the job in mind, too, at the same time.

127

"When Jerry asked about it a few months later, I'd got a new box in the meantime and I couldn't, for the life of me, think what had become of the coat. 'It's well on the way, Jerry,' said I. 'I was planning today how to tackle the job, and once you have a clear plan of campaign in your mind the job is as good as done. The whole secret of turning is the planning, so that you will make the best of the good parts of the cloth.'

"When he had gone, I asked herself had she any knowledge of it at all. 'Wisha!' said she, 'the ould coat? Why, it is in the window of the fowl-house. The boards of it are broken, and the fox might get in.' Good enough! the weather was warm, and Jerry wouldn't be in need of it for a while, and if I took it from the window, I would never hear the end of it.

"We had a spell of rain some time after, you remember, and the thatch on the oats was poor, and I slung the coat over it. That would be out about October. In December we had Jack of the Roads in to us for the night, and I threw the old coat down over him on the settle. Happen the next day, when he had gone, I started on it, and I had only a few stitches done when who should walk into me but Jerry himself.

" 'I'm glad to see that you are on with the coat, Tailor,' said he. 'The days are beginning to get cold, and I was thinking maybe I would be buying a new coat.'

" 'Have sense, man,' said I, 'keep your money in your pocket. There's years of wear and warmth left in this coat, and it's well on the way now.'

"I don't know what turned me from it. Someone came in, I suppose, and I put it aside on the settle, and herself tidied it away, and it went out of my mind altogether. The next time that I saw it would be in February. You remember the cold nights we had that February? Herself put it on the bed as an extra covering; and I can tell you that it was a warm covering. There was the best of stuff in it. Anyway, it was thrown idle, for I had a bit of work done on it, and you couldn't use it as a coat until I put it together again.

"When we threw it off the bed I was missing it for a while, and one day I thought that I would finish the job. I asked Ansty about it. 'Jerry Mac's coat? The divil fire you, didn't you give it to the Slater the night he was here, and it was raining and he had to go over the hill back into Kerry?' It was true for her – but how could you let a man go through a wet night with ne'er a coat on his back, and a coat idle by you? No Christian would do the like of that.

"So it sojourned for a piece in Kerry. When it came back to me, it was at an awkward time. It was the time I was having the head made, I think, and I had no time for the coat. When I came to take it up again, I was thinking that it would need a bit of alteration, and I would need to take the pockets off it to strengthen some of the worn parts of it. I sent word to Jerry Mac, as I wouldn't like to alter it unknown to him, and I put it on one side till I heard from him.

"What with one person and another coming to me through the summer, I had scarcely a moment's ease to myself. I took it down again in the autumn. Blast it! do you know what happened then? Jerry Mac sent a message up by one of his gossoons telling me not to trouble about turning the coat, but would I start making a 'habit' (shroud) of it for his waking, as he had just turned his fiftieth year! The goddam son of a bitch may the devil blast him the poor fellow's dead now may the Lord have mercy on him! – did he think I had nothing else to do but be turning his coat for him?"

Throughout the recital Ansty has remembered the beginning of it all, and when the Tailor has finished, she takes up the thread of talk where the Tailor's song held it.

"Better come away with me tomorrow," she says to the man of the worn trousers, "I'm going to go to Bantry. You can get the new pants, and we can drive the divil of a shpree together. There is to be a great auction sale. They are selling all the stuff from the forts, and I am going to buy a bed. Grand beds they are with the fine shpring mattresses."

"You will not, woman," interrupts the Tailor with vigour. "No bed from that sale will come into this house. I have told you before a thousand times, and I mean it."

"Why so? What harm would they be so long as they are good and cheap?"

"I tell you 'No,'" repeats the tailor with vehemence.

"They are better beds than you would get elsewhere."

"No matter. No matter if they have diamonds on them. You have been told that you are not to bring any bed of them in here."

"You and your old 'witchappery'! Why not? I tell you they are grand beds."

"And I tell you they are not. They are soldiers' beds."

"What harm in that so long as they are strong and cheap?"

"All the harm in the world, I tell you."

"'I tell you. I tell you.' Anyone would think you were the Pope the way you do be talking. What harm is there in soldiers' beds?"

"I've told you before, woman, but you are so stupid that you cannot understand. There is as much sense in your head as meat on a bone when the dog has done with it. They are infected, and I will not have the likes of them in this house."

" 'Infected.' Wisha! will you listen to him? What infection would soldiers have compared with human beings? 'Infected' . . . Glory be! . . . 'Infected.' . . . Leave me alone with him and his 'infected'. . . . It's infected yourself you are."

Ansty has succeeded in her object of riling and rousing the Tailor. There is a glint of victory in her eyes.

"I have told you a thousand times this blessed day that you are not to bring one of those beds in here because they are infected. But you are a stupid and an ignorant class of a woman, and you cannot understand. Soldiers, I tell you, have queer diseases, which you know nothing about, because you have not travelled, and do not know the world as I know it; and you argue with your ignorance. I tell you that soldiers have diseases you have never heard of – things like 'gunnery and erysipelas'."

"Glory be! . . . 'Gunnery and erysipelas.' " . . . The power of the word has temporarily stunned Ansty. She starts a period of fire-gazing and extracting the full benefit of these mysterious words by repeating them. "Gunnery and erysipelas! . . . The Lord save us!"

The Tailor recovers his equipoise. General conversation breaks into a hum again.

Attention surges from one to another; from the Tailor to Ansty; from topic to topic. Soon Ansty gets tired of talk. She has got the party spirit. She wants music.

"Come on, Johnny. Give us a song. We are tired of the talk. You always had the grand songs and the grand voice for singing them."

"Yerra, no. I have no voice at all, Ansty. The Tailor will give us a song. We haven't heard him for a long time now."

"The divil much you missed. The divil mend him and his songs. You may as well be listening to an ould frog in a ditch as listening to him singing."

"Come on, Tailor. Come on," says a chorus of encouragers. "Give us the Ticky-Tack-Too, or the Herring, or anything at all. Then Johnny will sing afterwards, won't you, Johnny?"

"I will. I will. Follow the Tailor's lead is good enough for me ever."

The Tailor fixes his eye on a succulent piece of bacon hanging from the rafters and starts.

> I've a herring for sale,
> From beginning to tail;
> Sing abero fain, sing aberum ling,
> Sing abero fain, sing aberum, sing.
> And indeed I have more of my herring to sing.

What do you think I made of his head?
As fine a griddle as ever baked bread.
Sing abero fain, etc.

What do you think I made of his eyes?
As fine a football as ever did rise.
Sing abero fain, etc.

What do you think I made of his throat?
As fine a pipe as e'er you did smoke.
Sing abero fain, etc.

What do think I made of his back?
A hardy boy and his name it was Jack.
Sing abero fain, etc.

What do you think I made of his belly?
A lovely girl and her name it was Nelly.
Sing abero fain, etc.

What do you think I made of his tail?
As fine a boat as ever did sail.
Sing abero fain, etc.

Sing boat, sing throat,
Sing Jack, sing back,
Sing Nelly, sing belly.
Sing abero fain, sing aberum ling,
I have no more of my herring to sing.

Men get up from time to time, and bid "good night". Newcomers take their places. Some stay all night. Others just drop in on their way to the shop, or on their journey home.

From each visitor Ansty endeavours to extract a toll in the form of a bit of gossip.

"Is it true that Bina Carey was at the doctor's on Monday?" she asks a near neighbour of Bina. "Whatever carried her there at all?"

" 'Twas nothing at all," replies the questioned one. "A bit of a sore throat, that was all I heard."

"A bit of a sore throat!" Ansty repeats incredulously. "A bit of a sore throat!" she repeats again, this time with sarcasm. "And she married six months last Shove, and nothing more the matter with her than a bit of a sore throat. And to be going to the doctor. A bit of a sore throat me eye."

"And why couldn't she have a sore throat as well as anyone

else?" asks the Tailor, with concealed innocence. He has a score to pay already.

"A married woman, these twelve months, going to the doctor with a sore throat?" challenges Ansty.

"It could be sore; why wouldn't she go?"

"Thon amon dieul! have you a splink?"

"Perhaps it was like the time Michael Raferty went to the doctor. He was a fierce drinker, and drank all before him. At one time he was a wealthy man, but he drank himself out.

"The doctor examined him and could find nothing at all wrong with him. He asked him questions about himself. Had he a headache? Had he a pain anywhere at all? But he had no headache and no pain. The doctor was puzzled and scratching his head. Wasn't there any help he could give him? Had he a sore throat?

"'Thon amon dieul! Of course I have a sore throat, but I wouldn't heed that at all. Why wouldn't I have a sore throat, when two public-houses, and two farms of land, and mountainy land at that, have passed down my throat?' "

"Always the shtories," remarks Ansty, and immediately grabs at her bit of fading gossip again. "I'll bet Bina Carey had no sore throat at all, but another sort of pain in her. And why not? Wasn't she married twelve months? It was time for her so."

"Oho!" chuckles the Tailor, "it was more like the case of the man who took his wife to the doctor in the old days. When the doctor took out his horn they had in those days for sounding a person, the man said, "Sound her well with your horn, doctor. Sound her well with your horn.'

" 'The divil a need,' said the doctor to him, 'by the looks of it you did that yourself long ago!' "

Ansty is not amused. She is still musing on the mystery of the sore throat. "Married twelve months and going to the doctor with a sore throat. Humph! a likely thing to happen."

"Come, Johnny, you promised us a song. Sing us the bachelor's song, and take our minds away from all the cares of married life. That is a grand song, and I like to be hearing it."

The song is sung and applauded, and the focus of attention breaks up again. There are half a dozen conversations going on at the same time. Neighbours are discussing the affairs of the day's work. There is a group leading Ansty on. The Tailor is explaining something or other.

Suddenly Ansty's voice cuts like a sword through the babel of voices.

"Did you wind the clock?"

"I did not," replied the Tailor in a colourless and matter-of-fact voice.

"Better wind it and then talk."

The clock is taken from its case and handed to the Tailor, who winds it solemnly without ever troubling to look at its face. It is returned to the box and the lid is closed. Time has been honoured, and life takes up its beat again.

"—'Pon my soul, I never heard the like—"

"—a curious class of people. They are called Minnetropolists, and they walk in their sleep, and can do all manner of things when they are asleep—"

"—and himself had a letter from him the other day—"

"Where is he now?"

"Yerra! he's away out in Boshton, in America."

"He is not in Boston," corrects the Tailor, who always keeps one ear cocked for Ansty. "He is in Chicago."

"Well, so. Where's that?" challenges Ansty.

"It is in America," the Tailor informs her.

"Didn't I say that he was in America?"

"You said he was in Boston."

"Isn't that in America?"

"It is.'

"Gon rahid! What do you contradict me for so? Didn't I say that he was in America? You're going cracked in the head with the old age and all the shmoking."

"Have it your own way so," assents the Tailor with the resignation of a philosopher. "There is no one thinks that they have the head so well by them as the mad people. And there would be no wise people if there were no fools."

"Come on, Tailor. Let's have another song. You are both right. Sing the 'Buttermilk Lasses'."

The Tailor needs no pressing. He settles back, and takes a deep breath and starts.

Come all you young fellows, whoever you be,
Draw nigh with attention and listen to me
It's on the new fashion I'm going to dilate,
That is worn by the buttermilk lasses of late.

Those donkey-bred girls, they must imitate
Each fashion that's worn by the ladies of state.
Their hair they embellish with ribbons and toys,
In order I'm sure for to please the young boys.

And every old woman that has got a dame,
She employs her whole efforts to keep up the game.
She sells them the eggs for to purchase a veil,
And pledges the blanket if all else should fail.

133

The sour buttermilk they sell by the score,
To purchase a cape or a silk parasol.
It's a jacket and bustle they then must provide,
And a pair of clasped boots their coarse ankles to hide.

For fear they are not in full show to be seen,
They must get a silk bonnet in red, blue and green.
You would think in your heart without a word of a lie,
That with ribbons and feathers they're ready to fly.

The finishing strokes are the brown bonny hats,
And the hair decorated with ribbons and plaits.
They're such numerous fashions it's hard to explain,
It fails my exertions them all to retain.

But the latest invention I almost forgot,
Which indeed is the strangest one of the whole lot.
The hoops which are worn, as I understand,
To make them both portly and stately and grand.

For to braze out the gowns, both of muslin and silk
That they purchase the same for the price of the milk.
No person on earth would imagine or think,
That they're fed on potatoes and sour buttermilk.

You'll see these young lasses on each market day,
With their boots in their hands and they trudging away.
To spare the light 'lastic that costs half a crown,
They don't put them on till they goes near the town.

It's then they do make a great show on the street,
Though at home they have beds without blanket or sheet.
Straw wads with a rug that's both worn and old,
And a cheap English blanket to keep out the cold.

Perhaps they have got but one shirt on their back,
And that without washing, both dirty and black.
And on each of their heels you will find a large kibe,
With a number of cracks that I cannot describe.

At home in the corner you'll find them each day,
With their heels in the ashes and they chatting away.
With the dog at the saucepan, the cat at the spoon,
The hens on the table, and the pig in the room.

Now to conclude and to finish with them,
I hope that these young girls will not me blame.
Because it's in order for to let them know –
That they're a laugh to the public wherever they go.

"Laugh to the public! ... Glory be! ... Hens on the table! ... The Lord save us! ..." So Ansty echoes for a few moments as she gazes into the fire, while the slow match of her thought burns. "Pigs in the room! ... Ring a dora! ... How long will it be till your pigs are fat, Jamesy?" she asks then.

"About another six weeks, Ansty. Are you thinking of buying one from me?"

"We could be doing with one soon. The one we have is nearly ate.... But himself should not be eating it. It's bad for him."

"Shouldn't be eating it! Who said I shouldn't be eating it? Pig's meat! Thon amon dieul! Pig's meat never did anyone any harm. It is the healthiest eating anyone could have. You could give it to a new-born babe. Shouldn't be eating it, indeed. Sure, we'll be buying one, and do you know that I have a fancy to cook it the way the Chinese do cook their pigs."

"How is that, Tailor?"

"They feed it up with all sorts of things. Snails and frogs and the best of oaten meal. Then they kill it and hang it from the rafters, and every man reddens a poker in the fire. The head manager of them gives a signal and they all stick their pokers into the pig. They have a kind of a song, in their witchappery of a language, as they stick the pokers in. 'Spongee for the mungee, johnee!' is how it goes. It is then that they have the grand eating and you should see the fine gravy that does run out of it."

"Hould, you divil.... Always the lies and the planning.... Snails and frogs!"

"What's wrong with snails and frogs? They eats them in France, and the French are the best cooks in the world. Because you don't like a thing you think that everybody else shouldn't. I tell you that there were better men and women than you brought up on snails and frogs. Didn't Napoleon beat the whole of Europe, and he ate nothing else but snails and frogs?"

"I don't know about Napoleon," answers Ansty disinterestedly, "but put a sod of turf on the fire, or we will all be as cold as frogs. You and your Napoleon!"

So throughout the evening the ball of banter is tossed about the kitchen of Garrynapeaka. A word brings a song or a story from the Tailor, and all his stories end with a bubble-pricking comment from Ansty. Nothing matters beyond the compass of the gleam of the fire. Cork is a long way away. The rest of the world is so far that it is forgotten. The hours speed by, until at last there is a shuffle of chairs.

Someone is making a move.

"Yerra, what hurry's on you?" asks the Tailor with indignation. "The night is young yet. Sit down and take your aise, and don't be making a slave of yourself to an ould clock. The world is only a blue bag. Knock a squeeze out of it when you can. I remember in the old days, there was a man by the name of—"

Chapter Eighteen

"It was a dark and stormy night. Two men sat by the fire at midnight. One said to the other, 'Tell us a tale.' The other began, 'It was a dark and stormy night. Two men sat by the fire at midnight. One said to the other. . . .'"

"I was talking to Tady Joe today, and he tells me that he has a notion to dig up that big 'gallaun' (monolith) that's on his land, and see what's under it. . . . Mwirra, but I warned him not to have anything to do with it," started Cork Echo.

"Yerra, why not?" replied the Tailor at a venture, to see what it would prompt in Cork Echo.

"Because there's no good ever comes of it, Tailor, that's the reason why."

"Tcha! That's all old superstition. What harm could there be in an old stone? If I had one in my place I'd soon dig it up, you may be bloodyful certain that I would."

"And if you did, you would never get the better of it. Something would happen to you as sure as today; mark my words."

"That's true for you, Cork Echo," chipped in Ansty. "To listen to him sitting on his backside beside the fire . . . and talking . . . you'd think that he was the bravest man in the whole of Ireland. . . . Cows in Kerry have long horns."

"Well, what harm can an old stone do you, I ask you?"

"The powers of the devil, Tailor. The powers of the devil."

"I declare to God but the two of you are a queer class of Christians. You'd think to listen to the two of you that no one else has a bit of the hand in running this world but the devil. The devil this. The devil that. The powers of the devil! The powers of me foot, more like," replied the Tailor with deep contempt.

"You can laugh and say this and that, but you can't go against what is. My father used to tell of an Englishman who had no religion at all, who dug up a 'gallaun' at Rossbeg years ago, and do you know what he found there, and what happened to him?"

"He found a power of money and lived well ever afterwards, and had pig's meat every day of his life, and a jug of punch going to bed at night."

"Mwirra, no. But the body of a giant! And there was a bottle beside him, and on it there was a notice printed, 'Give me three drops from the bottle.' "

"Well, and did they give him the drops?"

"They did not. They buried him up again – quick. Do you know that the Englishman died the following year?"

"Am bostha! You wouldn't expect him to live for ever, I suppose! Did they carry the bottle?"

"They did not. They covered it all up again."

"The more fools they. They had a right to carry the bottle. Do you know what that was? Like as not it was the 'Danes' drink', made from the honey of the heather. It was the most powerfullest drink ever known. Yerra, talk about your whiskey and your 'first run'. They were only walking after it. Do you know that one drop of that would keep a man young for a year? Doesn't it stand to reason if three drops would bring a giant back to life again? Thon amon dieul! What great fools they were, and all because of an old stone, and a lot of old nonsense, and the talk of ignorant people. These old stones are only headstones, such as you would see in any graveyard. That's all they were. They were only put there because there was a class of artists going in those days called 'bodysnatchers', and it was to stop their little game. But I don't suppose that you heard tell of those either?"

"Mwirra, but I did; and I know what they wanted the bodies for, too."

"Glory be! ... Dead people's bodies! ... What would you want a dead body for at all? ... They must have been the queer people. ... The Lord save us!"

"They were queer people, Ansty," explained Cork Echo. "But they had their own good reasons for wanting the bodies. They used to sell them to the manufacturers; and do you know what the people they sold them to did with them? ... They made castor oil out of them. The finest castor oil."

"Castor oil! ... The Lord save us! ... and to think they wanted them to make castor oil," Ansty mused.

"Castor oil! Castor oil!" The Tailor scarcely knew how to express his contempt. "A fat lot you know about it. They used to grind them up with dried cabbage, and make coffee out of them. The best coffee ever yet any man tasted. It was as rich as duck soup."

"Duck soup? ... Duck soup? ... Out of dead bodies? ... Hould, will you? There's nothing but the lies and the shtories out of the shmoke. ... Duck soup, am bostha, and this morning you were compla-a-aining and compla-a-aining and compla-a-aining in the bed, as though you were like to die ... but now

138

the laughing and the laughing and the laughing. Hould, will you, you and your duck soup?"

"That's the reason they had the headstones. It was only natural. After people had spent a deal of money on waking a man and burying him, they didn't see any sense to someone else coming along and making a profit out of him."

"It was castor oil," persisted Cork Echo like a bulldog.

"It was coffee, I tell you."

When at last the Tailor had battered Cork Echo down to silence if not acceptance, he continued: "There were a lot of other reasons besides, in the old days, why people had to be careful with graves, for the old people had some queer 'pishogues'. I remember to hear tell of people who carried butter from their neighbours, and how they did it was by the power of the hand of a dead person put under the churn.

"There's a great deal of power in a dead body, though you wouldn't think it. 'Tis something like the power for evil there is in prayers said backwards. 'Tis said, and I'd give credit to it, that no mill would grind for you until you had put a living Christian through it. I saw a trial of it myself, years ago, in a place near to Kenmare."

"Mwirra, but I wouldn't give in to that. 'Twas a barbarous thing to do."

"But you'd never give in to anything. You're one of the most contrairy class of a man that I know. I tell you that I've seen a trial of it myself. There was a man built a mill, and a damn fine mill too, near to Kenmare; and the people brought their corn to him to be ground. He put it into the mill, but it came out exactly as he put it in, and he was near off his head with the worry why the mill would not grind for him.

"Then someone told him of the plan to set the mill working, and he got an old omadhaun of a fellow and he put him through the mill, and ever after that it ground the finest ever you laid eyes on; and it does to this day. I saw the mill, working away, with my own two eyes, every day that I went to school."

"Thon amon dieul! But Tailor, that was an unchristian thing to do – to grind a living Christian in a mill!"

"Manalive, what harm? He was a man who was no good to himself, living, but always in his own way and everyone else's, and look at all the good he did dead."

" 'Tisn't right, all the same. 'Tis 'murder' I call it."

"You call it! You call it! If the world was to listen to you it would be in a queer state! If everyone in the county starved for the want of flour, wouldn't that be a bigger class of a murder? Have sense, man."

"Ground him alive in a mill? . . . The Lord save us, but it's an awful world . . . and was he dead?"

"Dead! the divil a fear but he was dead, when the crushers had finished with him. He was the finest meal-man meal!"

"Glory be!"

"But I remember a story about body-snatching which happened near to Kilgarvin, years ago; and it was told to me by a man who used to go the roads in those days. A fine, airy class of a man by the name of Ballsey. A man full of fun, and good for living and all kinds of sport.

"Well, he called in some night on his route, to a man he knew who was a kind of steward in a big house there at that time. They had the tea, and talked and smoked by the fire for a while, and then Ballsey said that he would sing a song. He was a grand singer, and had hundreds of songs, and was always glad to be singing. But the steward said 'No', as the man of the house might not like it, as his wife had died that day.

" 'Thon amon dieul! Why didn't you tell me before?' said Ballsey then. 'We'll go to the wake, so. When all fruit fails, welcome haws.'

" 'Yerra,' said the steward, 'there's no wake. The man is a bald-headed Protestant, and doesn't hold with wakes or any decent funerals. Just put her in a room, and lock the door, and eat his supper, and away to bed with him is his idee.'

" 'He must be a mean-spirited man,' said Ballsey, 'not to treat his wife decent. He needs teaching a lesson.'

"Well, no more about it that night, and they made the best they could of the situation, with no song and no wake, and when the time came they went to bed. The next day the woman was buried in the graveyard, which was adjacent to the man's land. The husband ate his supper, and away to bed with himself and didn't seem to care.

"That night Ballsey got up in the middle of the night, and he opened the grave, and he took out the body, and he tied it to the door of the house. When the husband came down the following morning and opened the door, the wife fell into his arms.

"I tell you that he got a start, thinking that he had seen the last of her. He got a weakness. They buried the body again that day, and that night Ballsey opened the grave and took out the body again. This time he tied it to the back of a pony which used to be grazing in a paddock under the man's window.

"The following morning he looked out of the window and saw the wife again, astride the pony, and galloping round like mad. He had another weakness, and Ballsey went to him with some brandy. When he was out of it, he asked Ballsey what could be the meaning of this, that she should be coming out of the grave.

Ballsey explained that it was because the poor woman thought that she had been badly treated, because she had not been properly waked, and that she would probably continue the habit so long as the man lived, and wherever he was she would find him out.

"He didn't like the idee of this at all, and asked Ballsey what he could do about it. Would it do if he waked her now?

"'No,' said Ballsey, 'that would not do at all. It was too late now. He was afraid that he would have to put up with the state of affairs. There's only one thing that you can do,' said he then, 'but it is a terrible thing for any man to have to do.'

"'What's that?' asked the man.

"'You'll have to sit by the grave tonight, and when she tries to rise out of it you will have to beat her back. But it will be fierce work, for they do have the devil's own power and strength. You'd have to take a good strong ash-stick with you. But if you manage to keep her down for tonight, which is the third night, you'll never have sight or sound of her again.'

"'I couldn't do that for a hundred pounds,' said the man.

"''Tis a terrible thing for a man to have to do,' agreed Ballsey, 'but if she comes out tonight you are ruined for ever. She'll be able to come out every night for the rest of the future. You'll never get rid of her for all your born days. She'll be worse dead than she was living.' He put a proper fear into the man, and in the end the man asked him if he would do it for him, which was what Ballsey wanted.

"'You're asking a deal,' said Ballsey. 'I doubt if any man in the history of the world has had such a job offered to him.'

"'I'll give you fifty pounds,' said the man.

"'It would be cheap at that price,' answered Ballsey. 'I might lose my health in the struggle.'

"'I'll make it a hundred,' said the man.

"'That's more like talk,' said Ballsey, 'but even then a man would not have to be in his right senses to face a job like that.'

"'I'll give you a gallon of whiskey, so,' said the man.

"'Make it two,' said Ballsey, 'and we'll call it a deal.'

"The man agreed.

"Well, that day Ballsey collected a bag of cats, and when the dark of the night came he took them to the graveyard and put them, still in the bag, on top of the grave. He was thinking that maybe the man would come to see that he was getting the value of his money, and right enough he did. As soon as Ballsey saw him coming he started at beating the cats in the bag and himself screeching, until there was the hell's own row, for a bag of cats would make a fierce row. Ballsey yelled and cursed all that he knew.

"The man saw that he was earning his money and did not want to come any closer than the railings, and away with him, satisfied, to bed. When Ballsey had finished the job of journey-work and knew that the husband had gone to bed, in with him to his friend the steward. I tell you that the two of them waked the woman decent with the two gallons of whiskey.

"The divil a stir was there from the woman in the grave after that, and the husband went away and got himself another· wife, and never another thought to the old one."

"Wisha! And to listen to him planning the lies, and the holy Christmas nearly here!"

"Bad luck to the lie is it! That's what happened, word for word, as Ballsey told it to me. But you people who haven't travelled and are ignorant make a wonder of these things. That's nothing at all. 'Tis only like a daisy in a bull's puss to a man who knows the world.

"When I was in Cork I was in lodging with a fellow who was studying to be ordained a doctor, and many and many was the night he would come home with a bag over his shoulder full of bones. After the supper we would turn them out on the table like a pit of spuds, and make a skeleton of them between us. Then we would fasten a cord to his spine from the joists and another to his legs, and the doctor would play the melodeon, and a damn fine player he was too, and I'd teach the skeleton to dance a jig.

> *Rise upon Sugan,*
> *Sing upon Gad,*
> *Shuffle, me lad,*
> *Both Sugan and Gad!*

"And you should have heard the fine clatter he used to make on the linoleum with his bare bones!"

"Hould, will you! . . . Did you wind the clock?"

"Better wind it, so."

And Mortality gives place to brother Time.

Chapter Nineteen

There was an air about Cork Echo as he came into the Tailor's on this particular evening. He closed the door with slow deliberation, as a man bearing great and important tidings. In his face and his whole bearing was the implication that he was "inflated" with news. But then it was nothing strange for Cork Echo to have news, and it was always important news. Yet tonight there was a difference. Whatever it was it was greater than the last occasion, when he had borne the tidings that the Garda barracks was "infested" with fairies.

He took his seat by the fire. The usual tuning up for the night's performance took place between Ansty and himself; the *hors-d'œuvre* before the more substantial fare; exchange of complaints, minor questions and answers. That part of the business settled, he crossed his legs, took the pipe out of his mouth and spat into the heart of the fire. Then he turned to the Tailor with challenge.

"Did you know Jimmy Paddy of Ballymacool?"

"Jimmy Paddy? What, the son to Paddy of the Patches? A great stupid block of a bosthoon of a fellow? A proper galoot, if ever a galoot walked the face of this earth? Thon amon dieul! but you may be sure I do, and his father before him. Many is the piece of a night his father and I—"

But Cork Echo was not in a mood for reminiscences. He brought the curtain down abruptly with another question.

"Did you hear at all that he came into money? Two hundred pounds?"

"I did not," admitted the Tailor, "but that could be, for he had an uncle who went to Australia, and he could have died and left him a legacy."

"Well, this was no legacy," Cork Echo thrust curtly, with the power of his undisclosed information.

"No legacy and came into money? ... Two hundred pounds?" Ansty voiced the problem and mused over it for a moment. "Was it how he was knocked down, and killed by a motor-car and got damages?" she suggested then.

"It was not," replied Cork Echo with scorn.

The Tailor backed him up.

"Yerra, talk sense, woman. Two hundred pounds for Jimmy Paddy, and fat pigs only eighty-eight shillings a hundred! It was found money, of course."

Ansty and the Tailor wrangled out the side-issues involved, and Cork Echo sat by and bided his time, for he has them both on strings tonight. When the heat of the side-issues had been dissipated he continued.

"It was no legacy . . . or damages . . . or found money," he declared. "It was how he won it from a newspaper for 'cross-words'."

"Oho! a libel action, was it?" perceives the Tailor, as a man well acquainted with the law.

"Mwirra – it was not," spat Cork Echo. "It was for winning a competition against all Ireland."

"Winning a competition! The divil blast it, but it must have been a competition to find the stupidest man in the whole of Ireland so," suggests the Tailor.

"It was not then," asserts Cork Echo in defence of his grand bit of news, which seems in danger of being ridiculed even before it is accepted. Drawing a newspaper from his pocket, he unfolded it and held it out and pointed to the news.

"There you are. In black and white for all the world to see. 'Third prize winner. Mr James Murphy, Ballymacool, Co. Cork. Two hundred pounds.' Now will you pay attention?"

The Tailor pondered over the announcement, a little stunned by it, trying to find the flaw in it. Ansty accepted it and tackled it as an established fact.

"Two hundred pounds! . . . Glory be! . . . Mister James Murphy! . . . The Lord save us! . . . Mister James Murphy! . . . Ring a dora! . . . Um! um! um! . . . I expect he's wearing a collar and tie now."

The Tailor looked at the announcement again and sat back and continued to ponder on the problem. "Now why the hell should any newspaper give Jimmy Paddy two hundred pounds?"

"Jimmy Paddy!" exclaims Ansty in amazement. "Jimmy Paddy, indeed! . . . Mister James Murphy, if you please . . . with a collar and tie on him."

"It was how he had some hold over them, and they had to give him the money, but I wonder for why."

"Mwirra – won't you believe what's printed?" asks Cork Echo, almost pathetically. "He won the money in 'a test of skill and intelligence'. Here it is, and here is what he did, printed plain." He pointed a gnarled finger at the item again.

Again the Tailor studied it, and again he sat back baffled. There was some mystery about it. "I'd like to have a look at that in daylight. They print these papers too faint nowadays to be read properly at night."

Ansty intercepted the paper on its way back to Cork Echo. She gazed at it blankly for a moment until her eye lighted upon an advertisement. Then she sprang up as though she had been stung by a wasp.

"Thon amon dieul!" she exclaimed. "Will you look at this!. 'Tis no wonder that the world is as it is, and that the hens are not laying, and that the tea is scarce, and there is no meal in the mill. . . . Will you look at that one, with ne'er a stitch on her but an ould corset! . . . Glory be! . . . and to see the make of her and the cut of her! . . . The Lord save us, but 'tis an awful world and the women being photoed in nothing but their corsets."

The Tailor took the paper back and glanced at it. "A fine make of a woman," he decided, cocking his head gallantly on one side. "A man could do worse than have the likes of her about the house in the idle time of the winter."

"Hould, you divil! 'Tis your beads you ought to have and you making jokes and laughing, and you almost in your grave."

"In my grave!" snorts the Tailor. "In my grave, indeed! It's jealousy, that's what's the matter with you. There was a man I knew of ninety-seven and he—"

The horse is running away from Cork Echo. Violently he wrenched it back.

"Mwirra – will you hould, both of you, with your women and your corsets and your carry-on! Do you realize that we are throwing money away? There is money going begging, and the likes of Jimmy Paddy come along and pick it up, while the likes of you are talking and blathering away."

"That's the truth, sure enough," agreed the Tailor, reduced to the serious contemplation of the situation. "Ansty, will you hould your whist! You'd better go away to bed for yourself. Now what is it all about?"

The Tailor drew a little nearer to Cork Echo. Ansty subsided, but did not go to bed. The night was still too young and held too many possibilities for that.

"Since Mary brought the paper up with her on her way from school the two of us have been studying it," explained Cork Echo. "Mwirra – but that girl is a great scholar. She'll get into the Civil Service one of these days. We make out that you have to tell the paper the right words for certain meanings. Cross-words they call them."

"That's easy enough," agreed the Tailor. "I've often thought that the people who printed the papers had not much of the headpiece by them. They want some good strong curse words, I suppose?"

K

145

"They do not," replied Cork Echo impatiently. "There's not a curse word amongst them. They are all simple words like 'Beam' and 'Pull', according to the list Jimmy Paddy sent in to them. There they are."

Cork Echo handed the paper to the Tailor again. He studied it for a moment, but then his eyes wandered.

"She hasn't much of the 'lumps of temptation', as Carty the Weaver used to call them," he commented after his study. "But there are few of the women nowadays who have. They can't suckle their children at all. It fails most of them even to breed at all."

Cork Echo snatched the paper away in disgust. "Mwirra – there's thousands of pounds waiting to be taken, and all that you can think of is a shameless woman."

"Shameless! Yerra, what has she to be ashamed of? It's only a sort of spite would say that. Fair's fair. She's a fine-looking class of a woman, as the women go nowadays."

Threateningly Cork Echo started to fold up the paper. "Will you pay attention to me and leave your women alone? Do you want this money, or have you too much of it? Thousands of pounds, and all that you are interested in is a shameless woman. There's a test of skill and intelligence, and all that you can think of is the lusts of the flesh."

The Tailor settled down again to take it seriously. Cork Echo appealed to his proper pride.

"I said to myself today that, if only the Tailor and I put our heads together, we ought to be able to do much better than Jimmy Paddy. We ought to get the first prize at least. Jimmy Paddy was never much of the scholar. Two heads are better than one."

"True for you!" agreed the Tailor at last. "Now tell me again what it is we have to do."

Cork Echo explained it all again.

"Strike while the iron's hot!" said the Tailor. "We'll settle the business right away and put them out of their pain. Ansty, get the pen and the ink and the paper!" The "table de hote" was taken down. The wick of the lamp was raised. "More light, manager. More light! We can afford the light of a penny candle to make a couple of thousand pounds."

A candle was lit and placed on the table. Ansty brought the ink-bottle. The Tailor dipped into the bottle with the pen, and brought up the body of a dead fly impaled on the point of the nib.

"Do you know that there is a curious sort of a cussedness in flies. To think that a fly should go to all the trouble to find my ink-bottle when he wants to commit suicide while there is a lake of sixty acres not half a mile away, and it teeming with trout, mad for flies. Yet this fellow should go to all the trouble to drown himself here when he might have been doing a trout a bit of good."

"First it's corsets, then it's women, then it's flies! Are we ever going to make this money, or are we going to be laughing-stocks for all the rest of our born days to people of the like of Jimmy Paddy?"

Now the Tailor's *amour-propre* was roused. He took off his hat. "The brain needs air for thinking." He took a firm grip of the pen. "What is it that they want to know?"

"The first word is – 'Found at water's edge,' " read out Cork Echo.

"Found at water's edge? . . . Why, the shore, of course."

"No. That won't do. It has to be a word with four letters in it, and the two in the middle are 'o' and 'a'."

"Yerra, that only makes it easier . . . 'o' and 'a'? No. It couldn't be 'duck' . . . . Why, manalive, it's 'boat', of course! Give me the paper, while I write it down."

"Mwirra – at first you won't move at all, and now you're like a cow that's gadding. 'Boat' won't do either. I said it was 'boat' to Mary, but she said that it was 'foam', and like enough she's right, for she's a great scholar."

"Wellso, where else would you find a boat? You wouldn't look up the chimney for it, would you?"

"And where would you find foam? You wouldn't look up the chimney for that, would you?"

"Thon amon dieul! have you ne'er a splink of sense at all? and you the man that has often dipped your nose into it. Wouldn't you find foam on top of a pint? And would you find a boat there? You haven't got this thing right at all. Boat it is."

"I tell you you're wrong!"

"I tell you I'm not wrong!"

In the middle of the argument which followed the door opened, and in walked the Sheep. The disputants barely noticed his entry. Ansty, who had sat silently after her repression, now had someone with whom to share the fun.

"Will you look at my two clerks, with their pens and their ink and their 'witchawatcha'. 'Tis 'crosswords' they do be at, making a thousand pounds. We'll have the divil of a night when they get it, and I'll be in the jug. It will be better than any wedding or any wake that ever was."

"Boat's the boyo!"

"I say it's foam!"

"God give me patience!"

"Mwirra and all the saints!"

"I've travelled a good piece of this earth, and I've met a deal of men in my time, but for the height of stupidity. . . ."

"They do say that a mule is obstinate, and I've had dealings enough with them, but never yet, in all my born days. . . ."

Then the two noticed the Sheep and made appeal to him.

"Yerra, here's the man of all the learning. Wouldn't you find a boat at the water's edge?"

"You would, I suppose. . . . Yes, I suppose you would, if it was there."

"Wouldn't you find foam at the water's edge?"

"Yes, I suppose you would. . . . Yes, I suppose you would, at times. But . . . what is it you're at?"

The competition was explained to him.

"I have no head for puzzles. They do say that they are dangerous things to be at. I have heard tell, but I don't know if it is true, but I did hear that it was puzzles that drove Michael Carey off his head, so that he had to be put away. I don't know for sure, but that is what they say. . . . Is there any news about the war or anything in the paper?"

"It's true for you," agreed Ansty the Philistine. "Not that the two of them want much driving. They are half cracked already."

"News! News!" snorted the Tailor. Then his eye lighted on the advertisement again. "There's no news at all except that there is a fine-looking woman advertising for a man, and she has her photo printed. She would do you grand."

Attention went back to the advertisement, to Ansty's delight. The Sheep gazed for an instant at the place where the Tailor's finger pointed. Then he drew back, as though an adder had hissed at him. He gazed at each of them in turn, wondering which was the devil which had put this temptation before him. Ansty rubbed the situation home.

"Isn't it an awful world? . . . No wonder the hens are not laying, and there's foot-and-mouth disease, and a war. . . . Glory be! . . . and to think that any woman would do that. . . . Cork Echo, you ought to be ashamed to have the likes of that in your pocket. . . . The Lord save us! . . . What would happen to you if you were struck dead on the road, and like as not you would be with that. . . . Ring a dora. . . . 'Tis an awful world."

Cork Echo was touched to the quick.

"How the hell was I to know that was in it? I bought it for the competition."

The Sheep put in his spoke. " 'Tis a temptation from the devil. That's what it is. A temptation from the devil. I have often heard tell of such things, but never before seen such a thing. Mark my words. No good will come of it."

"A temptation from the devil! . . . Glory be! . . . What is the

148

world coming to at all? ... and to think that any woman would be photoed like that.... The Lord save us! ... I'd die with the shame."

"Thamwirrashimfaina! and who the hell is asking you to be photoed like that, I ask you? There'd have to be no other woman left living before they would ask you. 'Pon my soul, but you old spears beat the band. You have nothing in your heads but jealousy and evil thoughts. Whenever a decent, goodlooking woman comes along, you all get together and spit at her like a pack of she-weasels. It's jealousy. That's all it is."

"A temptation from the devil, I tell you, Tailor."

"Temptation, me foot. Anyway, it's Cork Echo's paper. He brought it into the house. Perhaps he's the devil."

"How was I to know that there was such a thing in it? I bought it for the competition."

" 'Tis the way the devil works," declaimed the Sheep. " 'Tis the way he works. Tempting your soul with money. That's what he's doing."

"Mwirra – we'll have no more to do with it, then," decided Cork Echo. " 'Tis a bad paper would print the likes of that, and the money would be bad, and you could not tell what harm it would do the man who won it. We'll have no more to do with it."

"By the mockstick of war! but you're the most curiousiest pack of articles that I've ever laid eyes on. First you are mad one way, and then you are mad the other way. Has Jimmy Paddy gone to hell? The divil a fear. You may be bloodyful sure that he hasn't. I'll bet for a wager that he's raising a pint to his lips at this moment in John Murphy's pub out of the money he's won.... Fiddlesticks! I'll take the money myself."

Cork Echo was on the horns of a dilemma, torn 'twixt God and Mammon. "But if it's bad money, Tailor?"

"Bad money, me foot. No money's bad money, if you have it. Besides, if it is so," he added as an afterthought, "can't we get the priest to bless it? Isn't that what they are there for?"

Cork Echo's conscience was eased a little at this, and the two clerks set to work again. The Sheep withdrew to the other side of the fire, out of the way of temptation. Ansty mused and soliloquized.

"Bad money.... Glory be! ... and to think that any woman would be photoed in her corsets.... 'Tis an awful world.... The Lord save us! ... I suppose they won't even be wearing those next."

The argument broke out again.

"Boat. Foam. Foam. Boat."

Suddenly it ceased. The Tailor drew himself up like a judge.

"You're right. Foam it is," and he stuck the pen into the bottle.

Cork Echo was staggered at the Tailor's collapse. It was the first time for years that the Tailor had ever admitted himself to be wrong, and Cork Echo did not know how to tackle the novel situation.

The Tailor wrote in the missing letters, with the body of another fly stuck on the point of the pen. The ink made two large blots where the letters should have been.

"Didn't I say when you told me that Jimmy Paddy had won a competition that it must be to find the stupidest man in all Ireland? Well so. It isn't brains you need for this, but the height of stupidity. That's why it is 'foam'."

What with the moral onslaught and the Tailor's capitulation, Cork Echo failed to notice the backhandedness of the compliment, and the rest of the puzzle was soon filled in to his liking. He left it to the Tailor to post, as the postman did not call his way on the morrow.

"There'll be sixpence to send with it," he pointed out, poking a finger into his waistcoat pocket.

"The divil fire it!" said the Tailor. "Hold your money. What is sixpence out of a couple of thousands? We can settle that up when we get the money."

"Mark my words. It's a temptation from the devil," was the Sheep's parting shot. "A temptation from the devil offering you money for your soul. 'Tis the way he works, in innocent disguises."

The next night Cork Echo was kept at home watching a sow which was farrowing. From that he caught a cold himself, and was away for several nights. He came again the night before the result was due, and sat, content with anticipation, talking of minor details. Much water had flowed under the bridge of Garrynapeaka in the meantime.

"Anyone would think that you had the world of money, Cork Echo," remarked the economical Ansty, "the way you do be cracking matches and the fire before you. Hand him a piece of paper for his pipe, you," she commanded the Tailor.

The Tailor turned to the Office behind him and tore off a piece of paper. He twisted it to a spill, and lit it in the fire, and handed it to Cork Echo. Cork Echo lit his pipe with it. Then he quenched the flames between his fingers, and gazed at the stump of a spill as he drew the smoke. Suddenly his gaze grew intent. He unrolled what was left of the spill and scrutinized it, and then looked up at the Tailor.

In accents of anguish he asked, "Mwirra – so you didn't send the competition at all?"

"Competition? Competition?" For the shade of a moment

150

the Tailor was mystified and fumbled. Then he remembered and recovered, and answered with confidence.

"I did not. 'Twas a big temptation right enough, but I resisted it. Do you think that I want my name associated with the likes of Jimmy Paddy, or anyone who would sell their souls to the devil? 'Tis right enough, as it is written in the Book – 'What does it profit a man to gain the whole world and suffer the loss of his immortal soul.' "

The mention of Jimmy Paddy reminded Ansty.

"When will 'oo be getting the thousand pounds from the newspaper, Cork Echo?"

That was the straw which broke the camel's back. When the door had closed behind Cork Echo, as he went out bitterly into the night, Ansty asked, "What ails him? Is he sick? Has he a pain in his belly?"

"Pain in his belly!" laughed the Tailor. "You may say he has. 'Tis how he wrote to the woman of the corsets, asking her to marry him, and she wrote back a letter to him telling him how she was married already."

"Glory be! ... The woman of the corsets! ... Ring a dora.... 'Tis an awful world.... Who'd have thought that about Cork Echo, now? ... The Lord save us! ... You don't know what will happen next.... No wonder the hens are not laying.... Ah! Ah! Ah!"

Chapter Twenty

"I see how Seamus Murphy has taken up a contract to put up a statue to the four Kerry poets in Killarney," said the Tailor, ignoring the headlines of the news, and lighting upon something personal.

"One of those, and the greatest of them, was Owen Roe, Owen Roe O'Sullivan. The rest of them, O'Donoghue, Ferriter, and O'Rahilly, were only walking after him. He was one of the greatest poets that ever was. It's no use for anyone to be talking. They were all poets in those days, every bloody man.

"But that was not all about Owen Roe. He was an auctioneer as well, and he was middling good as a doctor as well. He was good enough at every trade. He spent a part of his time in the Navy, and was at the battle of Waterloo. But do you know what was his best trade, after poetry? It was making small lads.

"He was one of the most frolicsome men that ever was. It was said of him that if he threw a copper over a fence it would, like as not, fall on the head of one of his own. He must have been as good as King Solomon almost.

"One day a young gossoon met him on the road, and Owen spoke to him for a while, and then he gave him a penny, telling him that the next time that he saw him he would give him a shilling. Well, by the mockstick of war, what did the young lad do? He hopped over the fence and ran over a couple of fields and was there on the road before Owen Roe again.

"'You said that you would give me a shilling the next time that you saw me,' said he.

"'True for you,' answered Owen. 'Here is the shilling, and another for your intelligence. You must be one of my own.'

"Owen and the priests did not get on any too well together. Many is the time they had a battle, and Owen did not always get the worst of it, for he was a powerful and a barbarous man with his tongue. All true poets are. It's a gift they have. They see things as they are, and have the power over words to describe things as they are.

"Though Owen did not get on well with the priests, he got on very well with the women. I told you that he was a frolicsome class of a man, and the women were clean daft about him wherever he went. It was over a woman that he had one of his famous battles with a priest.

"He was staying in the town of Mallow at the time, and he had committed himself with a woman of that town.

"On Sunday, after Mass, the priest asked, 'Is Owen Roe here?'

"Owen stood up and showed himself, and said that he was.

" 'Very well,' said the priest. 'I command you to leave this parish.'

" 'Whyfor that?' asked Owen, knowing well the reason the priest had against him.

" 'Because of what you have done with a woman of this place,' replied the priest.

"Owen thought for a moment, and then he spoke up.

" 'Good enough!' said he, 'but before I go I would first say this. Remember that it was on account of a woman that our first parents were cast out of the Garden of Eden; that it was over a woman that Samson lost his strength and the Philistines were defeated; that it was over a woman that the fierce wars of the Seven Branch Knights were fought; that it was over a woman that Troy was besieged and the long Trojan wars were waged; that it was over a woman that the misfortune came to King Lir; that it was over a woman that Caesar and Antony fell; that it was over a woman, Devorgilla, that the English first came to Ireland; that it was over a woman that England was lost to Rome; and that it is over a woman that I, Owen Roe, am forbidden the town of Mallow.'

" 'Hold!' said the priest to him then. 'We'll say no more about it. Mallow has misfortunes enough already. You'd better stay where you are, and let the women look after themselves, and you come and have the dinner with me.'

"That was one battle out of many that he had and that he won. On another day he was passing a priest's house with a companion, and there was a grand smell of salmon cooking coming out of the house. The two of them were middling hungry, and the companion said to Owen Roe, ' 'Tis a shame that we are starving and that the priest should have more than enough.'

" 'I'll bet you for a wager,' said Owen, who was always ready for a bit of sport, 'that I will both eat the dinner with the priest and put him to shame.'

" 'Done,' said the companion, and Owen set about the business. He knocked at the door of the priest's house and asked if he could see the priest.

" 'You cannot,' said the housekeeper, after she had looked

him up and down, 'his reverence is just sitting down to his dinner, and he said that he was not to be disturbed.'

"'But it is a very important matter,' said Owen then. 'Go up to him and tell him that I have a troubled mind, and that I want to know what should a man do if he has money found.'

"The housekeeper went up and told the priest, and came back and asked Owen inside.

"'The priest says that, if you wait until he has his dinner finished, he will answer your question, and he told me to give you this herring,' said she, putting a sprateen of a herring before him.

"Owen looked at the herring for a minute, and then he took it up on the fork, and he whispered to it, and then he put its mouth to his ear and listened. He had some sort of witchappery of talk. The housekeeper watched him, and then she went up to the priest again, and she told him of Owen's queer antics.

"'Go down to him,' said the priest, 'and ask him what he is doing, and why is he doing it.'

"Down went the housekeeper again, and she asked Owen.

"'Oh!' said Owen, 'I had a brother who travelled to foreign parts years ago, and I was just asking the herring if he had any news of him.'

"When the housekeeper told this to the priest, he thought that he had a simple fool to deal with, and would soon be able to settle the business of the found money.

"'Send him up to me,' he told the housekeeper.

"When Owen arrived in the dining-room, the priest told him what the housekeeper had told him.

"'You say that you can understand the language of fishes,' he said.

"'Yes,' answered Owen.

"'Well,' said the priest, 'I had a brother, too, who travelled abroad. Could you get news of him for me from your friend the herring?'

"'You had better ask that of the salmon before you,' answered Owen. 'He is a much bigger and stronger fish, and more used to priests and their kin than the common herring.'

"'You are a deal smarter man than I took you to be,' said the priest, thinking at the same time that he would have more trouble in settling the business of the found money than he thought at first. 'You'd better sit down and eat the salmon with me,' he said then, thinking that they might be able to come to some agreement over the money.

"They ate the salmon away together, and then he asked Owen to drink the punch with him, which Owen did. When the dinner was finished, and they had their bellies full, the priest turned to Owen.

" 'You sent up word that you had a troubled mind about found money,' he said then.

" 'That is true, I did,' replied Owen.

" 'Now how much money would it be that you found?' asked the priest.

" 'The divil a copper,' said Owen. 'I was only wondering what would be the case if I did find money.'

"He had the priest beaten, and put to shame, and had his wager won. I tell you he was the smart man, and the man who would beat him would be the divil of a man entirely.

"I'd advise Seamus to put up a good, strong statue to Owen Roe himself, and not be wasting stone on the others, for he was the smartest, wittiest man that ever walked the roads of Ireland. I wouldn't be at all surprised if I could not trace a relationship to him myself if I set my mind to it.

"He was a class of a doctor too. He was what they call in this country a quack doctor. That is a doctor that has all the old traditional learning, and knows how to cure, and does cure. The other class, that aren't quack doctors, have just the title of being doctors and little else.

"I am a natural quack doctor myself, but I have never practised. The more's the pity, for I see learning out of books and the old ways being forgotten and the people dying as fast as ever.

"There's a cure for everything if only people would have sense and understanding. God never sent a disease without sending the remedy as well. In the old days the people found the remedies about them – not in pills and medicines and such-like. It stands to reason that the cure for a man who is sick in Cork is not to be found in Algery, as people think nowadays. The natural remedy is in Cork. It is some sort of a herb, as the old people knew, for they used herbs. I have seen these cures used, and used well, and the people who used them living to this day.

"It was ever known that the best way to stop a cut bleeding was to put a spider's web to the place, and the next best thing to that was to put the droppings of a cut pig, a gilt, to the cut.

"There was a great cure in the droppings of a gilt. If you boiled them for two hours in milk, and then strained them, and drank the milk boiling hot, it would cure the diarrhoea.

"There was a disease in the old days called the 'running evil'. The cure for that was to go on a dry course, to drink nothing at all for three weeks, but to eat everything dry. Yerra, there were cures for all diseases, and little call for a doctor. If a child had 'the thrush', which was a common enough complaint, they would put the gander under a box overnight so that she was starving. They would put the child to bed, starving also. The following morning they would take the gander, without giving it food, and put its feeder into the child's mouth and that would take away 'the thrush'.

"A child would get the whooping cough. The cure for that was to give it the ferret's leavings. To give food to a ferret, and then to give what the ferret left on the dish to the child. Another cure for this was to go out on to the road, and to stop the first man you met riding a white horse. You would say to him, 'Man on the white horse, what is the best cure for the whooping cough?' Whatever he would say should be given to the child and that would cure it. It might be Indian meal stir-about or potatoes or bread. Any damned thing, whatever he said would work the cure.

"The best cure ever for pneumonia was to bury the sick man up to his neck in a dung heap, and leave him there overnight. The heat would drive the pneumonia away from him, and he could come to no harm, for it would be the warmest bed that ever he slept in.

"If you had a sore eye the cure for that was to get the milk of a woman, and to shake it in a bottle until you had butter made, and then you would rub the butter to the sore, and the sore would go.

"The way they had to cure the labour pains in a woman was to get her lifted by a man who had lifted a donkey in his arms as soon as it was foaled. The power came into him then, and remained in him.

"Another kind of wisdom they had was to be able to tell what ailed a man by feeling his pulse. The man who had this learning was known as a 'pulse doctor'. Another class of doctor in old days was a bone-setter. He would, most times, be a blacksmith. He could replace bones that had come out of place, and set broken bones so that they would heal, and there would be no weakness and no sign left. He could often, too, cure a disease which was not of the bones by the touch of his fingers. The power of healing was in his hands, just as the power of handling a horse is in one man's hands but not in another's.

"All this knowledge is dying out of the world, and the more's the pity. Now they have their pills and their powders and their injections, and what good are they? Can the people do the feats the old people could do? Can they lift a hundred of meal and walk with it, or lift a half-tierce of porter from the ground, or walk to Macroom and back in the one day? Pshaw! their pills and their injections! They want to go back to the old traditions, and have a bit of sense for themselves.

"There was a priest, years ago, who used to be a bit of a doctor. All the medicine he ever used was horse castor oil. One day someone came to him and asked him if he could do something for Jerry Mahony, who was middling bad. The priest questioned him, and gave him a bottle of the oil, and told him to give it to Jerry, and to come and tell him how Jerry was the following week.

"The man did as he was bid. After Mass the following Sunday the priest asked him, 'How is Jerry?'

" 'Yerra. Father, he's doing grand. He's had to wear a petticoat ever since he took the bottle!'

"I remember a story of the time when they first used 'the enemy' in this country. There was a man, by the name of Jim Donovan, sent for the doctor. The doctor came and had to operate on him in this way, for he was costive. When the operation was over he asked Jim, 'How are you feeling now, Jim?'

" 'I don't know how I am,' answered Jim, 'but do you know, doctor, I think that you have a queer sense of fun. I like fun myself as well as any man living, but sticking a kippin (stick) up a man's backside is no fun at all in my meaning of the word.'

"I never practised as a doctor myself, except in a small way; but I once did a bit of surgery. This is how it came about.

"There was a man, years ago, who chopped off a finger in a furze-cutting machine. He buried the finger in a bog, and marked the spot well. Years later, when he was dying, and knew that he was dying, he sent someone to the spot which he had marked, and told him to dig up the finger and bring it to him.

"The man did as he was told, and found the finger, and it was as good as the day it was chopped off, for a bog will preserve anything for ever. He sent for me to sew the missing finger on, for he did not want to be chasing about on the Day of Judgment looking all over the damned place for his bit of a finger. There was no telling what might happen to the place where it was buried in the meantime, and he wanted to be ready and complete on the spot.

"Well, however, the man died before the messenger with the finger returned, and I had to do the operation on the dead man. I sewed it on with waxed thread and made a good sound and neat job of it, that would last till he wanted it. There was divil a stir out of him 'while the job was in motion'. He was the quietest patient either I or any other surgeon operated on. He had the best anaesthetic of them all, death.

"And the best cure of them all is sleep, and the best preventative of them all is right living – hunger and good food, work and sleep, sadness and laughing. Neither too much nor too little of any one thing."

Chapter Twenty-One

One day a silent stranger will go down to the Tailor's. He will stand before the Tailor as a black shadow, and the Tailor will look up and recognize him.

"Thon amon dieul! . . . Welcome," he will say, after a pause, as he extends his hand. So the Tailor will meet Death, for that will be the silent stranger's name, in the same manner that he has met all the incidents of living, with spirit and a certain eagerness. "The time has come.`. . . May as well die in June as July. . . . There's no use for anyone to be talking. . . . A man must meet what is on the road before him." His last breath will be shared by a prayer and a quip.

From Garrynapeaka, through the parish of Iveleary, and the barony of West Muskerry, will spread a sense of shock. The activity of living will be stunned for a while. "The Tailor is dead!" People will not believe it, and will repeat it to themselves. "The Tailor is dead!" "The Tailor is dead!" The fire will have sunk out at last in Garrynapeaka; the glow of life in one who warmed the hearts of so many people. No more will people ask after the Tailor. Never again will the journeys past Garrynapeaka be gladdened by a word from him, or a trouble lightened by his consolation.

From Garrynapeaka, all over Ireland, to England, Scotland and America the news will filter. "The Tailor is dead!" Garrynapeaka and Ireland itself to many will have lost something that cannot easily be replaced. Ireland, to those outside it, will not seem to hold the lure it held. There will be a wound in the living of the many who loved him, and the many who only realized how much they loved him when it was too late, and they come to know that a man matters more than a place or a country, and that a man is dead. A man who inspired love, because he himself loved so dearly.

Singly and in couples they will come to the wake. They will come by car and by farm cart, on bicycle, and saddle horse, and on foot. Men will come across the wild mountains from Kerry, no matter what the weather, to take a last look at the Tailor, and to pay their last tributes. They will be hard men of the mountains, and they will come for love and not for duty. Tears will be near to their eyes for the loss of the man who was the centre of so much fun and so little harm. For the man whose eye was so lively, whose mind so quick, whose heart so big, whose hand so warm, whose giving so generous.

They will kneel and say a prayer beside him. They will smoke and drink and recall a memory of him. The sadness will be lightened by a laugh at some recollection of him, as this one recounts a story of his, and another remembers an apt saying of his. That is how he would have it. "Life is too short for a long face. You'll be a long time dead."

He will be shouldered by his friends in the last sad journey he will make. The earth will take him back, and there will be nothing left of him but the memory of him in the hearts and on the tongues of the many who, in differing ways, knew him. "Cornucopia" will become an old battered box, no more. "The Office" will be dispersed. The "table de hote" will be broken up. Ansty will not survive him for long. The thread of their lives is too closely woven. They lived by and through each other too nearly.

Maybe in some antechamber of the new life the Tailor will await her coming, so that they go on together, wrangling, arguing, but hand in hand – the Tailor and Ansty.

Whatever is to come, the Tailor will make the best of it as he did of life. He will soon discover that the new world is "only a blue bag. Knock a squeeze out of it when you can." Wherever he goes he will go smiling and will create smiles. He will be curious about all the details of it, and tender advice, and make comparisons, and regret the old days while making the utmost of the new. He will offer his help, and all that he has, with the same lavish generosity that he did while living. He will change an old cottage by his presence into something which is not in palaces.

They will go up the hill together. Ansty with quick, nervous steps, and the Tailor swinging along on his crutch, with the leg curled round it, and the white hazel stick in the other hand.

You can imagine them glancing into Hell as they pass.

"Thon amon dieul!" says Ansty, "will you look at my divil, and the great fire he has! You'd think that he had all the world of turf cut."

The Tailor will chip in. "Just a minute, sonny," he will say. "I will show you how to make a fire." And he will practise the old art again, and fan the fires of Hell with his black hat.

Ansty will still find some fault.

"Hould, will you? Blowing ashes and dust all over the place!"

"What harm!" the Tailor will reply, interrupting his puffing and his blowing and his wafting for a moment. There will be a twinkle in his eye. "Dust and ashes! Haven't I told you often before that God made dust and ashes to keep women out of mischief? And if you don't believe me you can ask Him yourself in a while, when we meet Him."

Then they will journey on to the gates of Heaven. The Tailor will describe it all to Ansty, as though he was very familiar with it, and Ansty will gradually envisage it all, as the possibility of "driving the divil of a shpree".

She will be awed a little by the golden gates. To the Tailor they will be a bagatelle, as though Garrynapeaka had always golden gates, and maybe a little better than these.

"It's too grand entirely," says Ansty, "we'll go round to the back."

"Round to the back!" the Tailor roars. "Thamwir-rashimfaina! and didn't I have an invitation to the President of Ireland's own garden-party, and there was no talk of 'going round to the back'. Pshaw! Is it some class of a tinker you think you are, with your 'going round to the back'?"

The sight of St Peter calms Ansty. Here is something within her range.

"Look at himself with the great whisker on him. I wonder would he stand me 'a half shot' if I asked him. He reminds me of Jerry Cokely—"

And that reminds the Tailor. Hobbling as quickly as he can, he goes over to the guardian of the gates.

"Did you hear tell of a man by the name of Cokely, Jerry Cokely, passing this way? Jerry, the greatest saint in Ireland – may the Lord have mercy on him. Would he be inside, do you think?"

St Peter may not remember. There are so many saints inside, and he does not remember this one on the calendar of saints.

"Wisha! He would not be on any calendar or almanac. He was a real saint, a right holy man, and a right good man for living, and a man who was full of fun."

St Peter opens the gates, and the Tailor and Ansty pass in. Ansty turns to have a slap, if she can, at "the grand man at the gate", but the Tailor hurries her on, eager to search for Jerry. At last he comes across him, and his eyes light up. He takes the old friend's hands within his own two big warm hands and presses them.

"Jerry, my boy. How are you? How are things with you? Come, we'll get a half-gallon and sit down together, and you tell me all the news, and we'll redden the pipe together, as we used to do. Conflagrate the pipe – Jerry, do you remember? – and smoke it in conjunction. Jerry, my boy, I missed you when you went, and I was lonesome without you. I never forgot you. There wasn't a day passed that I did not think of you, and it does my heart good to see you again."

The two friends will sit and talk and smoke and drink together. Ansty will wander off on her own, and keep returning, and picking up a piece of the talk, and echoing it, and orchestrating it as she used to do. Jerry and the Tailor will "get middling young again".

Then Jerry will conduct them round and show them the lay of the land. The Tailor will be very interested in everything, and be full of suggestions. The journey will often be interrupted, when some sight reminds the Tailor of a story or a bit he remembers for Jerry. Ansty will be awed but irrepressible. Out of long habit, she will give many a comment and "a relement" in passing.

The Tailor will refuse anything but his old patched and familiar suit. He may consider a halo for a while, as a new experience, but soon, in a fit of impatience, he will cast it from him. "A useless class of an article. What the hell can a man do with a contraption like that? It neither keeps his head warm nor keeps the sun off it. You might say it is a dangerous sort of a thing to be wearing. A man might very easily get sunstroke with a thing like that. Give me the ould hat."

Very soon the novelty of it all will fade for Ansty. She will feel so ill at ease. It is all very fine and grand, but there is something missing in it, Something missing – "Thon amon dieul! the cow!" And if Heaven is the place where all our aspirations are fulfilled, Ansty will get back her black cow, and her ducks and her hens, and the weather and everything else there was to complain about, and so be happy.

Gradually, too, Heaven will fade for the Tailor. He will find a chimney corner, somewhere in Hell, where there are fires again. Somewhere or other he will dig out an old box for Cornucopia. There will be a settle behind him with Carlo asleep under it, and a fire before him, and always good company – "down at the Tailor's".

Villon and Rabelais and Shakespeare and Montaigne and Chaucer will find him out, and drop in and bring along other disreputable characters like themselves, who cared more for life than for the trimmings of life.

They will swap stories and songs, and there will be much laughter and merriment, and the sound of it will float up the chimney to Heaven. Fresh heads will be poked in at the door. One of the first will be St Francis. Ansty will wipe a chair for him with a wet cloth.

"I heard the sound of laughing, and I couldn't resist

coming down. It is so long since I had a real laugh. Things are so perfect and respectable up in Heaven, and I find it a bit of a strain. You see they made me a saint. Do you mind if I sit for a while?"

"Yerra, man, you are as welcome as the day. Sit there till the backside wears out of your pants if you like. These are a few jolly cuppers who drop along now and again for a smoke and a chat and a song to pass away the time."

Ansty views the stranger with suspicion for a while. The Tailor greets him with a smile and the grasp of his hand, but he must pay his admission. The Tailor must have a kindly rub at him.

"But this won't do at all, at all. You'll be 'upsetting the balance of power', coming down here. Saints where sinners ought to be. Sinners where saints ought to be, and ten o'clock in the morning, and not a child washed in the house, as the man said long ago. But did I hear you say that you were a saint? I must tell you the story of Lollipopus, and how I nearly once made a saint myself."

Ansty will be full of wonder and respect for a while, and will view the stranger from a safe distance.

"A saint! Glory be! . . . What did he do to be made a saint? . . . A saint! . . . The Lord save us!"

After a while she will get used to his presence.

"Saint! Saint!" she will snort. "He's no more of a saint than the rest of the people who does be in and out here all day and all night. I'll bet it wasn't for talking they made him a saint. . . . Not a word of the talk. . . . More like an ould dummy or a budogue than a saint. . . . And he's a saint! Well, leave me alone with him. The queer way things are."

So the long days of eternity will pass. Rabelais will tell the story of the great discovery of the goose's neck. Chaucer will recount the reminiscences of the wife of Bath. Shakespeare will tell once more the story of the merry wives of Windsor.

"At Windsor? . . . Ring a dora! . . . That for 'oo! That was the carry-on. . . . Glory be!" Then Ansty will have a surge of respectability. She will turn to the Tailor, and cut short his laughter. "Better for 'oo to be saying your beads than sitting there with the shtories out of the smoke, laughing and shmoking."

"Yerra, woman, didn't I spend a lifetime at that, and where did it land us but into Heaven, and you had no cow and nothing in the world to worry about? Have sense, woman, for a piece. or we may find ourselves back there again."

The Tailor and St Francis will discover their common interest in animals and the ways of animals. and as soon as he talks.

Ansty will take to him and turn to him herself with questions. She will ask him if he is married, and how many small lads he has, and how many cows.

There will be the sound of the shuffling of a chair. Someone is making a move.

"Yerra, what hurry's on you?" asks the Tailor with indignation. "The night is young yet. Sit down and take your aise, and don't be making a slave of yourself to an ould clock. The world is only a blue bag. Knock a squeeze out of it when you can. I remember, in the old days, there was a man by the name of. . . ."

Epilogue

My first meeting with the Tailor was as the reader meets him in the first chapter of this book. Passing up the road by the side of his cottage I came across him, sitting on the bank, "minding the dairy herd". He had watched me, with his bright robin eyes, climb the hill, and as I approached him he greeted me with a warm interest and soon invited me into the cottage for "a heat of the tea" – the first of many hundred such.

Then I went on, up the remaining half mile of a rough winding road to "lone Gougane Barra", that then almost secret lake valley high up in the mountains bordering West Cork and Kerry. There was no inkling in my mind of all that was to spring from that seemingly casual-meeting. I returned frequently to Gougane for visits, and the casual meeting with the Tailor ripened into friendship. Years later, after much physical and mental wandering, I returned to Gougane to live there for several years.

I thought then that it was the peace and the beauty of the place which drew me back. I know now that it was the Tailor and Ansty which drew me. From then on, over the course of many years, no day passed that I did not visit them at least once.

On summer days I helped the Tailor in the all important duty of watching the cow. Stretched in the heather, we discussed the curious ways of the world, the strangeness of women and the cussedness of cows. I went for expeditions with him and to wakes and funerals. I shared gargantuan Christmases with him and Ansty. I suffered Ansty's scolding, particularly for my casual attitude towards fairies on my winter visits; and I was warmed by her charity, her solicitude and her generosity.

I was not alone in this thraldom to the old couple of Garrynapeaka. The Tailor's fireside was the gathering place for a host of friends, whenever they could manage it, not only from Ireland but also from England and America.

It was as a memoir for these many friends that I originally wrote *The Tailor and Ansty*. I had the opportunities of both leisure and a long-continued intimacy with them. I knew them in the winter as well as in the summer.

The memoir, in typescript, circulated amongst these friends and gained their approval. They criticized it only for its brevity and its inevitable incompleteness. It was then serialized in Sean O'Faolain's periodical, *The Bell*. Later it was published in book form by the highly respectable publishers, Chapman and Hall.

The publication roused the rancour of that small but active body of pharisees which exist in every country, driving them to ugly words and deeds and the banning of the book. The banning gave rise to a public controversy which eventually brought about the book's "unbanning".

But, long before this, the book ran out of print and, over the years, whatever copies remained from the holocaust were unprocurable, I myself was without a copy for many years until last year when I was able to see the book again in a xerographed form.

In the twenty intervening years since I wrote *The Tailor and Ansty,* I have frequently been asked to meet some old man "just like the Tailor". (I have never been proffered another such as Ansty.) With interest and a hopeful expectancy I met them. They may have had a fund of stories, a colourful turn of phrase and the countryman's shrewd wit, but none proved to be anything like the Tailor.

What then, I have asked myself, was it about the Tailor and Ansty which stood out and made them so different, so memorable?

In the beginning – and in this I believe that I speak for all who came to know the old couple intimately – I was drawn simply by the stories, the colourful speech and the wit. But very soon I found myself caught up in the life of Garrynapeaka, in the excitement and the swirl of unexpectancies, fashioned out of the simplest occasions. Later still, it was the warmth and the reality of their natures which held me.

More deeply I think that their friends sought them in order to be subtly and unconsciously instructed in that most religious life of the whitewashed cottage: in the daily and hourly gratitude for the very fact of being alive, expressed by a total immersion and acceptance of all aspects of living.

Against a background of poverty, of severe physical handicap and pain, we were shown – had we eyes to see – that life could be, and was, lived with an enormous appetite, gusto, gaiety, courage, and a certainty which made hay of the various religious, philosophical and political labels with which we buttressed ourselves against the real in our individual lives.

We were, in fact, privileged to participate in the lives of two people, near to the end of their lives, who had preserved still the innocence, the zest, the wonder and the faults of children.

That Johnny Con's cow had had a black calf; that Patsy Dan had received a letter that morning; that Hitler had invaded Russia, were all occasions for "Well, Glory be. Now that for 'oo!" from Ansty.

A hen crossing the road; the mislaying of his hat; the marvellous fact of waking up in the morning were, to the Tailor, all great and marvellous events, worthy of consideration and comment.

"Come day. Go day. God send another day."

"Take the world fine and aisy and the world will take you fine and aisy."

"The world is only a blue bag. Knock a squeeze out of it when you can."

"Imagination was given us not to make the worst of a good job. Any fool can do that. It was given us to make the best of a bad job."

"There's philosophy, and more than philosophy for you," as Joxer Daly might have said, and the life of Garrynapeaka was lived on these terms. A candle shining through the dark.

Epilogue II

LISTEN TO THE BANNED
A Pastiche

"Tailor, they have put you on the banned list."

"Yerra, there's no end to the honours. Now what band would it be? It wouldn't be the Quarry Lane band, by any chance, would it, for that was a right good band in the days when I was in Cork. Not like those queer confraternity bands and temperance bands . . . Temperance bands, moyah! . . . Did you ever hear the like?

"No, Tailor. I'm sorry but it isn't that kind of a band at all. The book is banned. It isn't to be sold any more."

"Whyfor so? . . . Is it how they have run out of paper?"

"No. I'm afraid that that isn't the reason."

"Well, it must be that everyone has a copy got. It won't be

long now before Ireland becomes the wisest country in the whole world when they all have it read."

"It is the law which says that it isn't to be sold any more."

"The law! ... That explains it so ... That's what you would expect from the law ... You might as well be trying to hang your hat on a rainbow as expecting sense from the law ... Haven't I had dealings with them myself. They only see the world upside down and back to front ... But tell me, what has the law got to do with the book?"

"The Minister of Justice has appointed a board of censorship. They read all the books and then advise him whether they should be sold or not."

"Thon amon dieul! You don't mean to tell me that they have invented another Board. Haven't we already more than enough with the Tourist Board, the Turf Board, the Pig Board, the Egg Board and the Warble Fly Board to plague us, and now you tell me they have got even another ... Do you know what it is? At this rate of progress we'll soon find ourselves in the strangest position any country ever found itself. We'll wake up one morning and find that everyone in the country is either in the government or on a board and they is no one left to govern."

The Tailor settled the fire and hung the kettle on the hook. The other half of the banned came in with a clatter of buckets.

"The divil break your legs! Whatfor have you the kettle hanging? ...'Tis only half an hour ago since we had the dinner."

"To cool it, woman. To cool it," replied the Tailor to the challenge.

Ansty stands aghast, bereft, for a moment only, of speech.

"Have you ne'er a splink left? To cool it, woman. To cool it. ... and the serious puss on him."

"Only following government orders, ma'am. The government decided this morning that there is to be no more sense in Ireland and in future the country has to be run on government lines. That's why I put the kettle on the fire to cool it."

With the peremptory air of a self-appointed Kettle Un-hanging Board, Ansty lifted the kettle off the hook and sallied out into the sanity of the fresh air.

"Tell me," said the Tailor after the interruption, "what's it all about at all?"

"The government have stopped the sale of the book because the Board think that it is 'indecent'."

"'Indecent. Indecent!' ... When I was in Scotland there was a man who got a gaol sentence for indecency, and rightly so, but, in the name of God, how could a book be 'indecent'?"

"The Board of Censorship has decided that the book is 'indecent' insofar as it is suggestive of or inciting to, sexual

167

immorality or unnatural vice or likely in any similar way to corrupt or deprave'."

"By the mockstick of war!'Tis like a mouthful of hot porridge ... 'sexual immoralitee', indeed! so the board read the book and that's what the poor fellows found in it so ...' Twas ever said that, search hard enough and be sure that you will find what you are looking for ... The man with dark spectacles sees all the world dark."

The Tailor poked at the sods on the hearth for a moment or two as he digested all this.

"'Tis a funny state of affairs when you think of it ... The book is nothing but the talk and the fun and the laughter which has gone on for years round this fireside ... Not alone this fireside but every fireside in Ireland for hundreds of years past and it took our own Irish government to discover that it was 'sexual immoralitee'.... our own elected Minister for Justice and his board of ould hairpins ... Did none of them, or the Minister himself, never sit at an Irish fireside at night and listen to and join in the talk ... or are they all but a pack of Dublin jackeens, aping the English.

"Many years ago there was a man came to this country to do it a great harm. He was a man by the name of Cromwell. A sour-faced divil if ever there was one. He would shoot anyone he saw smiling. Before he came Ireland was known the world over as a country of laughter and fun and sport of every kind. Cromwell came with his army to stop all that. That was a long time ago. But it looks now to me that he left a lot of descendants ... Yerra, when is the next election? ... You'll be down later for a piece of the night? but before you go let me have the bit of law gibberish again ... suggestive to or inciting to sexual immoralitee or unnatural vice or likely in any other way to corrupt or deprave ... Have I got it right ... I'll be wondering in the meantime was it the story of Johnny Con's sow which incited the board to sexual immoralitee or the bit about the tourist who didn't know the difference between a bull and a cow which depraved and corrupted the Minister."

That night the Tailor sang. He sang "The Buttermilk Lasses' He had a new concluding verse for it.

> *Now all you young maidens,*
> *Don't listen to me*
> *For I will incite you to immoralitee*
> *Or unnatural vice or in similar way*
> *Corrupt or deprave you or lead you astray.*

Eric Cross